C000220371

A peaceful old man kissed by his grandchild, a brutal murder in Northern Ireland, a road accident and a mummified corpse—do you find these images of death shocking or frightening?

the hidden certainty

Have you seen a corpse? How would you feel if you did? Considering how many people die it is surprising to find how few people have actually seen a dead body. For many of those who haven't, there is a real fear of what death looks like and how they will react to it. But this is not something we discuss: death is embarassing, questions about it are said to be morbid. We may be ignorant, anxious and curious about the subject, but to betray our interest is 'not nice'.

Unless a subject is freely discussed, it is hard to find words to discuss it with. That used to be the problem with sex— what words to use; the problem was partly solved by taking vocabulary which had been scientific into common language. Words like 'sexual intercourse' aren't specialised any more, people use them without embarrassment. For death the problem has yet to be overcome. For several reasons it is a subject cushioned by words which avoid the fact and try to soften the blow, resulting in some of the most hackneyed phrases in the language. 'He lost his wife'. Without thinking, it's very easy to ask where he lost her, and if he found her again but you'd feel a blundering and heartless idiot if you did.

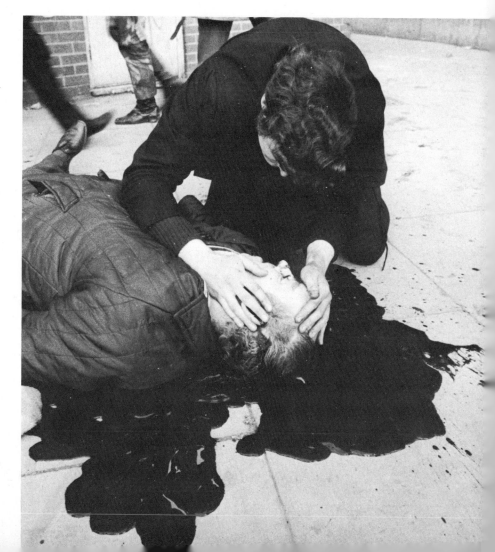

2

War graves in Northern France.

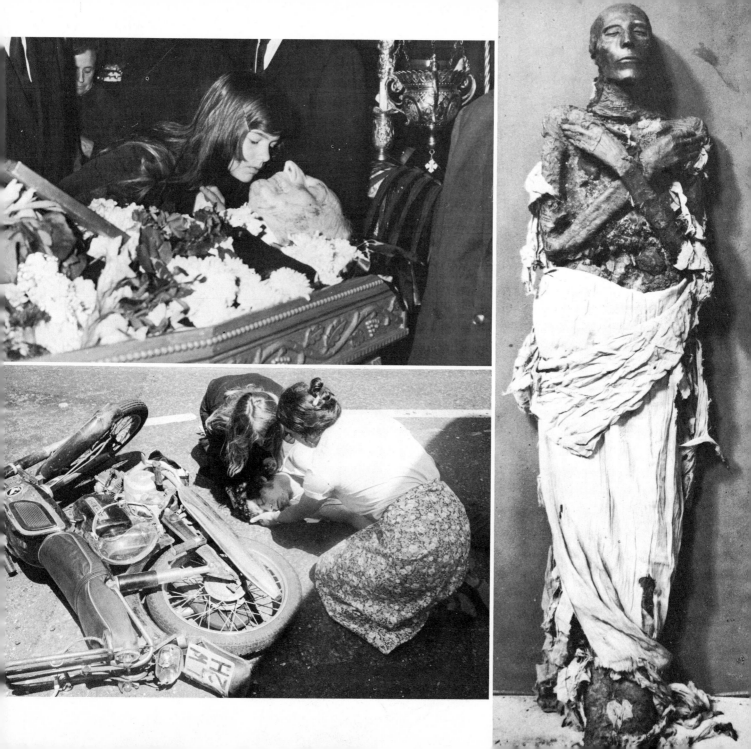

The most familiar expression is 'He passed away' or 'He went'. There are plenty of ways to say that somebody has died without actually saying it. These expressions suggest the same thing: that though he's gone, he'll be back. This is especially true of the common comparison between death and sleep. Dead people look like sleeping people, a fact seized with relish by poets, Shakespeare in particular. On many tombs we find the same quiet wish: *Rest in Peace.*

Vague and flowery language has helped to make death taboo. And ignorance of death has made it even more difficult to discuss. It is astonishing how hidden the facts of death are: behind the imposing fronts of institutions, the curtained windows of undertakers, the high hedge of the crematorium. These are not places to wander in and take a look. Plenty of writers have found it in their interests to play on our fear of the unknown and make death terrifying. Coffins and cemeteries and vaults are the stuff of the best horror stories, and it is enjoyable to have chills creeping up the spine sometimes. But in a way these tales, by making death macabre, have prevented us from considering it honestly and realistically.

Death is our problem. It is the one thing we know for certain, and we share that knowledge with everyone who is alive. It ought to be the subject of the best communication, cutting through national and age barriers. Certainly it has been the subject of great literature and art, which have overcome these barriers. But between ordinary people it is not a topic of conversation. Death isn't something you talk about with people you don't know well. And it's hard to bring it up with those you do know well in case they are frightened by it. You don't want to upset them.

This personal involvement in death is the real obstacle. It touches too many tender feelings. Yet not talking of it, surrounding it in flowery phrases and misleading old wives' tales, is perhaps more dangerous than ignoring it completely. Death is inevitable. It must be faced.

As with other subjects that make them feel uncomfortable, adults often make a rotten job of telling their children about death:

'I told her that Grandad had gone to Jesus in Heaven. I tried to make it as much like a fairy story as possible, without telling lies.'

'We told my son quietly that his Granny had gone away.'

'We told them that Nan had gone away for a long holiday and will not come back. She has gone to stay with Baby Jesus.'

'I told my younger son that Grandad was in a long sleep and was gone away to a happy land.'

'I told him that his Grandad was in hospital. I think he knows now but I didn't tell him.'

'I told them nothing. They never asked.'

Quotations from Geoffrey Gorer
Death, Grief and Mourning in Contemporary Britain

In America there are moves to hand over this responsibility to schools. It has been suggested that 'death education' be made a school subject, to be started as early as possible in a child's life, even in pre-school or kindergarten. So when you ask your Dad, he can say 'Ask your teacher'.

But while there may be some excuse for parents, and teachers, who are, after all, just more people who haven't seen a corpse, it seems extraordinary that many doctors also find this a difficult thing to talk about. The problem of 'to tell or not to tell' when treating a dying patient—this crops up constantly in medical journals. And how do you say it when you've decided to tell? Later in this book a nurse describes how doctors sometimes seem at a loss in this situation. After all, death is a sort of failure for them.

Perhaps the saddest inability is in ordinary people, not professionals. We seem to have lost the knack of knowing what to say and how to act when someone dies. A widow says of her friends and neighbours:

'They probably felt a little bit embarrassed; I'd have felt a little bit embarrassed. When I've met people before, I've thought: "Oh dear, what shall I say? Shall I look the other way?" and I think my neighbours have felt the same. . . I think people tend to be embarrassed if you speak to them; they feel they must say something, and they don't quite know how to say it.'

Geoffrey Gorer
Death, Grief and Mourning in Contemporary Britain

Censorship is usually associated with politics and sex, but death embarrassment has led to some subtle censorship in film and some, less subtle, on the radio. Don't laugh at this. I know that every night on the telly the corpses fly in some violent action, in story or on the news. But have you noticed that when the policeman in

the detective series is looking at the corpse in the morgue, the attendant always holds the sheet so he can see but we can't? And often a camera angle will make sure that the audience miss the corpse completely.

For a while the BBC had a policy of banning songs about death. These songs got plenty of air space on foreign stations and pirate radio stations though, and, despite the ban, made a significant impression on the hit parade. There was 'Tell Laura I love Her' where the hero died in a drag-car race. The thunderous 'Leader of the Pack' and the plaintive 'Terry' ended in motorcycle fatalities. One of the most successful of the songs of this kind was 'Ebony Eyes', sung by the Everly Brothers

to a catchy and sad country and western tune. It's about a young soldier waiting for his girl to fly out to marry him. But at the airport the news comes over the loudspeaker that her plane has crashed without survivors. Everybody waiting for that plane has to 'report to the Chapel across the street'. The final two verses are about how 'the ebony skies have taken Ebony Eyes' and how if the young soldier gets to heaven 'the first angel I'll recognise, will be beautiful Ebony Eyes'.

Sad or sick? Why do you think the BBC banned this song and others like it? And why do you think enough people bought it despite the BBC ban, to put it high in the hit parade for a long time?

How true is this comic-strip version of death in wartime?

Where people die

'He shouldn't have tried to blow them all out.'

People once died at home, nursed by their families and visited by their friends. After death they were prepared for burial by a relation or a neighbour and lay in the house where they died, watched constantly (for signs of life, mainly) until the funeral. As a result, most people had first-hand contact with death, and sometimes old people will tell you how they were taken, at a tender age, to see the corpse of a relation. On the whole they don't seem to have liked the experience much. It was with Florence Nightingale in the mid-19th century that nursing the sick and dying became a profession, and death began to move out of the home and into the hospital. Outside there is violent death on the roads and in working life, but this is a kind of death we will look at later. For the moment let's concentrate on 'natural death' from old age or illness. It is exceptional nowadays for a family to keep a very sick relative at home: they will receive more skilled care in a hospital. Consequently, 80 per cent of the deaths that occur every year occur in hospitals, old people's homes and other institutions.

This is a very convenient arrangement. People have jobs to go to. They can't just take weeks off to care for someone who might be ill for who-knows-how-long.

And those who don't have a job outside the home, probably have plenty of work looking after the rest of the family. And dying can be a messy and demanding business, involving cleaning and nursing of the most intimate sort. Most modern homes are hardly designed for the whole upheaval it would cause. Our ignorance of dying is partly the result of handing the business over to others because it doesn't suit us to do it ourselves. But there is a kind of emotional disadvantage to care by experts; many people need to show their love by caring for the sick person themselves, and find a fulfilment in the nursing which helps to offset their sorrow at the situation. And it is acknowledged that by caring for a dying person we do some of our mourning *before* the death, so that it is slightly less terrible to bear.

Cecil Day Lewis was a famous poet who died of cancer. He died in the house of his friend, Elizabeth Jane Howard, and here she describes what happened. Jill is the poet's wife.

'During these last six weeks, nearly all of his oldest and closest friends came to see him. The saddest exception was Rex Warner, not yet back from America. Otherwise he saw nearly all of those whom he loved best, and although he grew perceptibly weaker, his spirit remained undimmed, as clear, as gentle, as it had always been. He never complained, and he never lost a second's consideration for other people. He had times of great melancholy, almost despair, but he tried always to conceal them, except occasionally to Jill, who was the nearest and dearest to him of all.

On his last night it was Jill who called me. Her generosity in letting me share that vigil with her is something I shall never forget. We held his hands in turn, to love him through his dying. He died in peace, after his eldest son, Sean, had arrived, and one minute after Daniel got here from his school, slipped so quietly from us that for a moment we hardly knew. He said once that he did not fear death, but rather the act of dying. Perhaps for all his other kinds of courage and endurance, that night, at any rate, he was spared all fear.'

Elizabeth Jane Howard
How Day Lewis wrote his last poem

'The final cause of death is usually the failure of vital centres which govern the beating of the heart and the act of breathing. The practical question is the disease or injury which leads to this failure. In Britain in 1970 these diseases were:

Heart disease	130 243
Malignant diseases like cancer	109 342
Respiratory diseases like bronchitis (not TB)	69 023
Brain diseases	74 257
Motor vehicle accidents	6 453
Other accidents	9 682
Suicide and self-inflicted injury	3 753
Congenital abnormalities	4 211
Diabetes	4 353
Tuberculosis	1 465'

Black's Medical Dictionary

Dying at home is not such a common occurrence nowadays.

NO PARKING PLEASE FUNERAL

Many old people dread the idea of going to hospital, since they feel they will never 'get out' again. There is comfort to be found in familiar things when you are ill, and strange surroundings and faces can be very frightening. Have you ever been ill on holiday? It's even more miserable than being ill at home.

'The doctor wanted him in hospital, but he wouldn't go. He even got a bed for him. I stood and looked at him—he said, "What are you staring at me for?" I said, "I'm thinking what a lot they could do for you in hospital." He said, "So you're one of them—just thinking how soon you can get me out of my own house. Well I'm not going." The ambulance was due to come next morning, but he died during the night.'

A neighbour talking about a widowed man of 83.
Cartwright *et al. Life Before Death*

Of course, some old people are still left to die at home and the story is often an unhappy one as these newspaper accounts show.

'Twenty-four hours after her death the police found 78-year-old Miss Hilda Sampson sitting in a chair, still clasping the hot-water bottle she had filled in a last vain bid to keep warm.

News of the World

'Two elderly spinster sisters, who "kept themselves to themselves" starved to death in one of the most crowded areas of Glasgow. When Mary and Margaret Mellon were found in their top flat in Agnes Street, Maryhill, there was no food in the house. No fuel. And just 13 shillings—all in obsolete half-pennies. . .

Scottish Daily Express

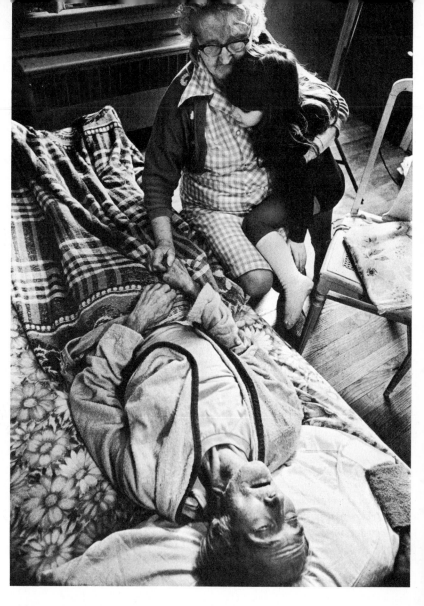

Wouldn't these people have been better off in hospital?

It is difficult and surely wrong to try to establish a general rule for how the very sick and the dying should be cared for.

Frank Tugend died amongst his family at home in Pennsylvania. His wife and children chose to look after him instead of sending him to hospital. As he grew weaker, the one thing he wanted was somebody with him. So long as one of his family was holding his hand, he seemed comforted.

Hospitals are clean and hygienic, and in an old people's home there is care always on hand. But some doctors feel that old people should be allowed to live out their lives in the surroundings they know with their personal possessions about them—even when this is quite squalid.

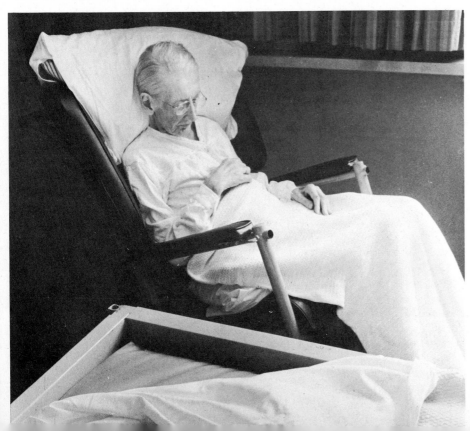

Every person should be treated as a special case in a way which best suits him or her. But this is not an ideal world and shortage of hospital staff and social workers, lack of concern from relatives, and the pressure of work and their own problems, all mitigate against personal and loving treatment.

'Our hospital is an acute hospital for the care of the sick rather than the dying. It always seems sad to me that a patient can be there in bed, dying, with so much life going on around. I've seen it again and again. In a busy ward everything is geared to people getting better. We've got an old lady at the moment in one of the side wards. She's quite conscious, and she gets her nursing care, but it would be nice if someone were there with her. You don't have the time though. One of the doctors said today, "I've really forgotten about her." He didn't mean it unkindly, it's just that there's nothing active to be done for her. In terminal care hospitals, that is, where people go to die, there are still doctors, but they're there to help the patients and to make them comfortable. In a general hospital dying can be a lonely business.

I don't know if the old lady knows she'll die soon. Not many people say they know, but I think you must get an idea. The word is avoided by all the doctors. If a patient says to a doctor "Am I going to die?" nine times out of ten he'll say, "Oh no, of course not." They won't often tell a patient if its a terminal illness either. I think sometimes the doctors are embarrassed about mentioning it.'

A nurse

Disasters

So far we have been preoccupied with the death of individuals. Large-scale disasters, particularly if they happen in distant places, are difficult for the mind to take in. What can statistics like these really mean to us personally?

- In May 1976, 1000 people were killed in an earthquake in Northern Italy.

- On 3 March 1974, 350 people were killed in the crash of a DC 10 airliner north of Paris.

- Between mid-1973 and mid-1974 in Wollo province, Ethiopia, 2 000 000 people died because they had no food.

- 12–13 November 1970: 1 000 000 people died in the hurricane which hit the Ganges Delta Islands of Bangladesh.

- Between April and November 1918 21 640 000 people in the world died of 'flu. 225 000 of these died in the United Kingdom.

After the Hochwald plane crash, where 105 people died, the coffins were put temporarily in a school gym.

There are some special hospitals in Britain where those who are dying can be nursed and helped together. The idea sounds rather grim, like those stories of tribes who leave their old people in the bush to die. But the reality is not like that at all. Because these hospices, as they are called, are set up to care for the dying, there's no question of patients being 'left out' and it seems that often they feel better and gain new interests in a hospice. Sadly there are very few, and as yet, they are all set up as charities. But perhaps the dilemma of where people die will lead to more pressure for such places to be established.

'Meanwhile the welfare officer at the general hospital had told me of a special hospital which had been founded with the purpose of easing any pain felt by long-term and dying patients. She gave me a booklet which was read to me by various friends and it was agreed I should apply to go there. I was enthusiastic at the prospect of a more comfortable and peaceful existence in the time remaining to me. Though I was at first advised I should be prepared to have to wait some time, on July 17th I received the good news that they could take me within the next two days. I arranged to go the next day and was elated at the prospect. . .

I continued to enjoy my remission to the best of my ability. An exceptionally kind friend gave me a present of a wine cooler which was further stocked with bottles by other friends. One of my greatest pleasures has always been to drink and talk with my friends. The hospital has raised no objection. Indeed, it has given positive encouragement to anything that might give me pleasure, and I was even allowed a visit from my cats.

Since coming to the special hospital I have felt a new person, for when I was at the teaching hospital I really felt close to death and considered taking something to end it all. Here I have been able to do things I thought I would never do again. This has been the most enormous pleasure, and I have enjoyed life once again.

Sadie Dunnet 'Dying of cancer' *Sunday Times*

A missionary doctor related perhaps the grimmest attitude to dying I ever heard. The mission hospital takes patients from an enormous area, a radius of 150 miles. Patients travel on public transport, which means a 'mammy truck', a Bedford lorry with wooden planks across the back, on to which the patients squeeze, six or seven to a row, fleshy and comfortable until the truck begins to move. The dirt roads, holed by heavy rains, make the journey a bruising misery for the fittest.

It costs a penny a mile to travel on these lorries. It costs 1000 times as much to hire one. Consequently, if the missionary indicates that a sick man is going to die, the relatives take him home immediately on the passenger truck, to save the cost of a whole lorry to transport his coffin. What must that journey feel like?

'One further submission, m'lud. May I be struck down dead on the spot if I'm not telling the truth.'

Dying young

At the present time, in Europe and America, most people are old when they die. There is something right and proper about dying in old age, when the prescribed 'three score years and ten' have been lived. News of such a death often receives the comment: 'Well, he had a good innings', or something similar. It does seem that as people grow older they view their eventual death more and more calmly. The body gives signals that it can no longer cope with the active life it once managed, and perhaps this is a preparation for the time when it can't manage any life at all. Certainly it is not uncommon for old people to be serene and accepting about approaching death, and contact with people who feel like this can be very comforting if death does frighten you. They don't find the prospect awful at all.

But the death of a young person is different. Nowadays it is quite rare, but one hundred years ago, four-fifths of all who died were under 65 years old. Infant mortality in the Western countries has been drastically reduced, and many of the diseases which killed children and young adults have been prevented or contained, so that accidents are now the main cause of young death in this country. But in a class I taught in Africa, *every* student had experienced the death of at least one brother or sister (which was the reason their parents had a lot of children: a sort of insurance policy).

In this passage an African primary school teacher has just learned of the death of a bright little boy in her class.

'I sat down thinking about him. I went over the most presumptuous day-dreams I had indulged in on his account. "I would have taken him away with me in spite of his mother's protests. She was just being absurd. The child is a boy and sooner or later she must learn to live without him. The highest class here is Primary Six, and when I am going away, I will take him. I will give him a secondary education. Perhaps, who knows, one day he may win a scholarship to the university." In my daydreams I had never determined what career he would have followed, but he would be famous, that was certain. Devastatingly handsome, he would be the idol of women and the envy of every man. He would visit Britain, America, and all these countries we have heard so much about. He would see all the seven wonders of the world. "Maami shall be happy in the end", I had told myself, "People will flock to see the mother of such an illustrious man. Although she has not had many children, she will be surrounded by her grandchildren. . . " I saw the highest castles I had built for him come tumbling down, noiselessly and swiftly.

He was buried at four o'clock.'

Christina Aidoo 'No Sweetness Here'
Black Orpheus

12

A HEART OF GOLD
STOPPED BEATING
TWO ...TTLE ...

MEMORY OF
KEITH
WILLIAMS
AGE 9.

CHERISHED
MEMORIES OF
...VIN THOMAS
JONES.
...LOVED ELDEST SON O...
ANN & ELWYN
APRIL 9TH 1957
OCT 1ST 1966

A SUDDEN CALL
FROM GOD ABOVE,
TOOK FROM US
ONE WE LOVE,
NO WORD, NO WARNING,
NO LAST FAREWELL,
DEEP IN OUR HEARTS
YOU WILL ALWAYS DWELL

...MEMORY OF
KEVIN
JONES.
AGE 9.

VICTIMS OF THE PANTGLAS SCHOOL DISASTER

W. MOSSFORD
ELY CFF

The disaster at Aberfan, in which 144 people including 116 children died, shocked the world. Money poured in for this memorial.

A final family photograph as a remembrance for this family in Chile where child mortality is very high.

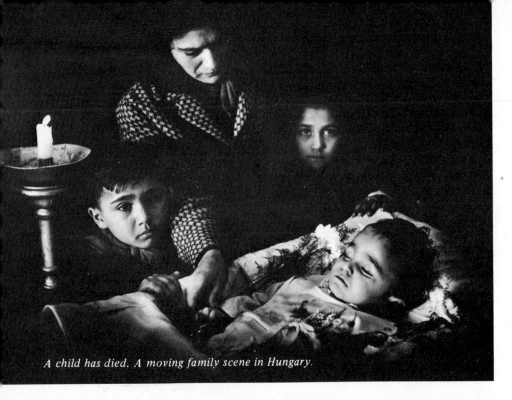

A child has died. A moving family scene in Hungary.

Why is the death of a child so awful? Why does it make us feel not just sad, but angry, too? Anger is a modern reaction to child death. In 1844 Elizabeth Barrett Browning could write:

' "It is good when it happens," say the children, "That we die before our time." '

This was a deep belief for the Victorians. Children were innocent, they hadn't had enough time to spoil their lives, so they went straight to a better life in heaven. Support for this view was, they claimed, to be found in the New Testament. And it was a belief that the Victorians needed, to console themselves, perhaps, when so many children did die.

Although it is much less common for us,

we still need mental defences to put up against the death of children. For mourners there are some 'consolations'. The mental image they will keep will be of a young and attractive person, not an old and tired one. Though this adds to the pain of the death in one way, it aids the idolisation of the dead person, which many people need to help them through their grief. The danger in this defence is that it can easily become maudlin and sentimental. The Victorians were adept at pictures of angelic little ones, about to depart heavenwards. But before you laugh at them, what about 'Love Story'? This best-selling book and money-making film told of a happy young marriage which ends with the death of the beautiful wife. This occurs in her young

husband's arms, and she manages to look very pretty all the time. A real tear-jerker. We like a weepie, and that's fine, providing we don't confuse sugary tales with the real thing.

It is understandable that people need to deceive themselves about the harsher realities of life. You may have done it yourself, pretending, for example, that your favourite pop star is not like other people—somehow better. When articles in the newspaper suggest that this isn't so, you don't believe them. Perhaps you have seen photographs or film of President Kennedy. His death illustrates another 'consolation'. He might have done fine things as President of the United States, but he didn't live long enough to do them (or fail to do them). So Americans can say 'If only Jack Kennedy were still in the White House. . . ' when times are bad. They are left with their dreams. The regret for what might-have-been has conferred the status of a legend on many who have died young, even when their achievement has hardly earned it.

In 1955 a film star called James Dean was killed. He had only made three films, in all of which he gave promising performances. Immediately after his death his fame grew and grew until eventually he was being acclaimed as one of the great stars—or as one who would have been one of the great stars, if he'd lived. Nothing could prove the claim wrong. In this way, a myth can grow around the memory of those who die young, and they acquire a kind of 'life'. Sometimes this is so real in the minds of admirers that they refuse to believe the hero is really dead.

The refusal to accept that death has occurred is a common part of mourning. But by the time the funeral is over, most people have passed beyond this disbelief into grief. When the death in question is that of a national leader, especially one on whom people have depended, it sometimes happens that they cling to his life and rumours circulate, often for years, that he is not really dead. The traditional model is King Arthur, sliding off into the mists on his barge, destined to return to his people once again. Old tales, you may think, and a thing of the past. Well, in 1916, when Lord Kitchener was killed, the unquestioning trust that people had put in him at the beginning of the First World War made it difficult for them to accept his death. As soon as the news was known, a story grew that he was alive, and had been sent on a mission so secret that the government had spread the story of his death to deceive the enemy.

When Adolf Hitler died in 1945, his death was followed by a crop of rumours, generally that he was in hiding and would return to lead the German people. Needless to say, the Allies squashed this story, since it might have developed into a dangerous political force. The same motive led the Bolivian authorities to exhibit the body of Che Guevara, the freedom fighter, after his death in the Bolivian jungle. Such was the power of his personality, and his past success as a guerilla, it was thought that only the sight of his bullet-wounded corpse would convince his followers that he was really dead. But was he? In the obvious sense, yes, but it is less easy to destroy the passionate ideas someone like Che stands for. In many ways a martyr to a cause can never be truly dead. Their fame lives on.

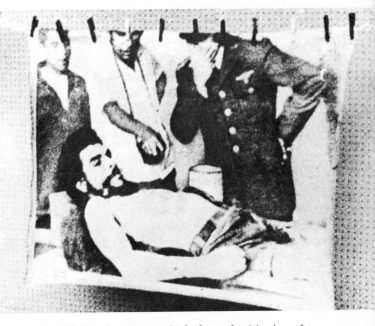

This is the picture which the authorities issued to prove that Che Guevara was actually dead. But posters with his portrait still sell all over the world with the slogan 'Che Lives!'

Tourists queueing for a fun-fair? Not at all, in fact this is a queue for John F. Kennedy's grave, visited by 10,000 people a day.

15

Dying heroes

War is the hungriest killer of the young. It requires a supply of young and healthy men, which is quite a responsibility for those who send the soldiers off to fight. We need especially tough mental defences against the death of the young in war. The Roman poet, Horace, wrote: 'It is a great and glorious thing to die for one's country.' Since then, and probably before then, too, people who send young men off to wars have made themselves feel better with the thought that the boys were being given the chance to die as heroes. John Masefield described young men setting off by sea for that slaughter-house, the First World War:

'All that they felt was a gladness of exultation that their young courage was to be used. They went like kings in a pageant to the imminent death. As they passed from the moorings to the man of war anchorage on their way to sea, their feeling that they had done with life and were going out to something new welled up in those battalions; they cheered and cheered and the harbour rang with the cheering. . . '

Those left behind made their contribution by writing pieces like this, by calling the carnage 'sacrifice', by singing inspiring songs about the brave young men. It was the folk back home who made the legends about the war, and when it was over they made monuments and stained glass windows, portraying young men of physical perfection. Heroes have to look the part.

Are the days of warrior heroes over? The nature of war has changed. Servicemen in Vietnam didn't feel they were dying for a fatherland. And while the young men who didn't enlist in the First World War were presented with white feathers as a sign of cowardice, the young men who refused to be conscripted for Vietnam were admired. Modern warfare involves everybody, not just servicemen, and it is waged with monstrously inhuman devices against which individuals don't stand a chance.

Veterans who escaped death in the trenches of World War I remember their experience in a dignified procession.

Right: *Those who died in the World Wars are remembered on a national scale in the yearly service at the Cenotaph. The Queen and the Prime Minister lay wreaths and the thousands of people who attend keep silence for one minute. Is it a real sign of respect to continue mourning for the dead like this? Or is it morbid?*

Left: *The real horror of war — a German soldier in the trenches in the First World War.*

Jan Palach, the student who publicly burned himself to death as a protest against the invasion of his country by Russia, gave a focus to the feelings of the whole of Czechoslovakia. The people of Prague file past his coffin and university professors in their gowns keep vigil.

The bodies of thirty-nine Israeli soldiers, listed as missing, were only returned to Israel after heavy pressure had been put on the Egyptian government. For many people who are bereaved it is necessary to have actual evidence of a death before it can be accepted.

Perhaps the new heroes are people like Jan Palach. He was a Czechoslovakian student who burned himself to death in 1967, in protest at the Russian invasion of his country. Apart from the sensational manner of his suicide, there was something about the character of Palach, generally unsensational and quiet, that made his gesture particularly moving, and he has remained a symbol of the fight against oppression. His grave was always covered with lighted candles and flowers, and students would sell his photograph at the gate of the cemetery where he was buried. These tributes so rattled the authorities in Prague that they dug up Jan Palach's body and moved it secretly. The flowers and candles are still brought to the grave that used to be his.

A soldier has just wounded an enemy soldier and now they are trapped together in a trench:

'It is early morning, clear and grey. The gurgling continues, I stop my ears, but soon take my fingers away again, because then I cannot hear the other sound.

The figure opposite me moves. I shrink together and involuntarily look at it. Then my eyes remain glued to it. A man with a small pointed beard lies there; his head is fallen to one side, one arm is half-bent, his head rests helplessly upon it. The other hand lies on his chest, it is bloody.

He is dead, I say to myself, he must be dead, he doesn't feel anything any more; it is only the body that is gurgling there. Then the head tries to raise itself, for a moment the groaning becomes louder, his forehead sinks back upon his arm. The man is not dead, he is dying, but he is not dead. I drag myself toward him, hesitate, support myself on my hands, creep a bit farther, wait, again a terrible journey of three yards, a long, a terrible journey. At last I am beside him.

Then he opens his eyes. He must have heard me, for he gazes at me with a look of utter terror. The body lies still, but in the eyes there is such an extraordinary expression of fright that for a moment I think they have power enough to carry the body off with them. Hundreds of miles away with one bound. The body is still perfectly still, without a sound, the gurgle has ceased, but the eyes cry out, yell, all the life is gathered together in them for one tremendous effort to flee, gathered together there in a dreadful terror of death, of me.

My legs give way and I drop on my elbows. "No, no," I whisper.

The eyes follow me. I am powerless to move so long as they are there.

Then his hand slips slowly from his breast, only a little bit, it sinks just a few inches, but this movement breaks the power of the eyes. I bend forward, shake my head and whisper: "No, no, no," I raise one hand, I must show him that I want to help him, I stroke his forehead.

The eyes shrink back as the hand comes, then they lose their stare, the eyelids droop lower, the tension is past. I open his collar and place his head more comfortably. . .

In the afternoon, about three, he is dead.'

Erich Maria Remarque
All Quiet on the Western Front

The instant of death. A photograph taken in 1938 by Robert Capa in the Spanish Civil War.

DEATH and the law

Changes in the law regarding death suggest that our general attitudes have changed a good deal recently. Take suicide. Before 1961, if you tried to kill yourself and failed, you could be charged with a criminal offence. If you succeeded, your body could not be buried in 'consecrated' ground. (Before 1882 a suicide was buried at a cross-roads, with a stake driven through the corpse.)

The law on abortion has changed too. Before 1967 it was a criminal act to end, or help to end, a pregnancy. After 1967 the ending of a pregnancy by a doctor became legal in most cases where it was wanted. Abortion may not be a question of death at all. It all depends on the way you consider an unborn child. Is it a human being before it is born, so that abortion kills it? Or is it a part of the mother, over which she has all control until its birth? The argument over this problem continues, but the law has taken its own stand and exists, I suspect, because of the same change in attitude which led to the changes in the law on suicide.

There is a third area of recent change. This was the abolition of capital punishment. It is a change that has provoked plenty of hostility, but again it seems to be related to a changed attitude towards killing and dying. The reasons for executing a murderer are several: so that he can't do it again; so as to frighten other possible murderers; so that we can punish with 'an eye for an eye'. But how valid are the first two reasons? 'An eye for an eye' is the nastiest aspect of capital punishment: it looks rather like an indulgence in the anger and self-righteousness that people who have never been tempted into a crime show towards people who have committed one. In this spirit, executions used to be public, elaborate, and dramatic occasions, with complicated apparatus as part of the ritual. There was a waiting time between sentence and execution, a kind of rubbing-in of the punishment. The pressure for abolition of hanging in Britain was speeded by the suspicion that mistakes had been made and the wrong men and women hanged. Many people seem to have been alerted to the full horror of the proceedings when these mistakes became known. But perhaps the greatest influence on public attitudes has been the growing understanding of psychiatric conditions. We have begun to appreciate that in most cases of murder,

Doctor admits mercy killings

A senior surgeon yesterday talked of the massive and fatal injections he had given terminal patients throughout his medical career — " but always at their own request."

Mr George Mair, who retired from medicine in 1968 but remains listed in the current Medical Directory as a Fellow of the Royal College of Surgeons of both Glasgow and Edinburgh, said he could not remember the exact number of people on whom he carried out euthanasia. "But it is not a small number."

Asked if he feared p tion, Mr Mair, aged 60 " This is at the back mind but I feel that the benefit from publicisin sort of thing is really to justify any anxiety feel myself."

the balance of the killer's mind is dis turbed. The last woman to be hanged this country, Ruth Ellis, would now considered to be suffering from 'diminished responsibility' and be re- prieved. At her trial in 1955, howeve was considered that since she looked calm as she committed murder, she r have known what she was doing.

'VEGETABLE' GIRL MUST STAY ALIVE, SAYS JUDGE

Machine cannot be switched off

From PIERS AKERMAN in New York

A GIRL whose illness has made her a "human vegetable" must be kept alive indefinitely, a judge ruled yesterday.

The judge in New York banned doctors and the girl's parents from switching off the machine that supports her shadowy life.

Karen Quinlan, aged 21, has shown no sign of brain activity for seven months. Her coma is believed to have been caused by a mixture of drugs and alcohol.

Superior Court judge Robert Muir said: "The hope of recovery is remote, but no doctor would testify there is no hope at all."

Karen . . . before her illness

On appeal, the Supreme Court ruled that the 'extraordinary means' used to keep Karen alive might be dispensed with. The mechanical respirator which sustained her breathing was removed—but she continued to survive, though she still required intensive care, oxygen, antibiotics, and special feeding.

These legal changes show a freer attitude towards death. Nowadays we can compromise, and tend to put the individual, his needs and difficulties, before inflexible judgements about right and wrong. We have been taught to recognize the shades of grey, rather than to see things in black or white. We may feel compassion for the suicide, sympathy for the mother who cannot want her baby, understanding for many murderers. But is this 'liberal' attitude wise? Does it bring out the worst in people, encouraging them to be thoughtless and irresponsible because they will 'get away with it'?

Some people are particularly worried about what they feel may be the next step. This could be 'euthanasia'. It means literally 'easy death'. The supporters of euthanasia point out that many people who are dying of painful diseases, often when they are old, would prefer to be gently killed by an over-dose of drugs given by a doctor, than to spend months in suffering, causing pain to all around them. This woman is a supporter:

'The man with a hopelessly damaged head kept "alive" on a respirator; the elderly cancer patient who contracts a pneumonia that, without antibiotics, will probably kill him; the paralysed spina bifida baby who, without an operation, is very likely to die, but will never be normal anyway—cases like these present new problems in decision-making that old adages about the "duty to preserve human life" do not cover.'

Gillian Tindall, *Observer*

Franco: how they keep him alive

ONLY an extraordinary exercise of will is now keeping General Franco alive—not his own but that of his doctors. Almost anyone else with a history of such acute illness at 82 would be allowed to die in peace.

As it is, Franco is receiving intensive treatment that is virtually unprecedented for a man of that age.

General Franco would almost certainly have died a week ago if he had not been attended by a team of 26 specialists at a cost of something like £3,000 a day. On Friday night he had his second major operation to remove most of his stomach to stop heavy bleeding. He was given 12 pints of blood during the four-hour operation to remove bleeding stomach ulcers.

Even our most advanced medicine can't keep death at bay for ever. General Franco died on 20 November 1975.

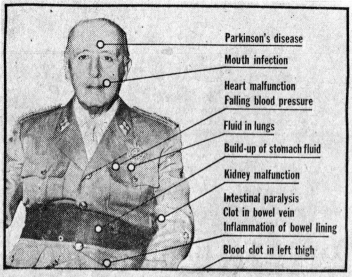

Parkinson's disease
Mouth infection
Heart malfunction
Falling blood pressure
Fluid in lungs
Build-up of stomach fluid
Kidney malfunction
Intestinal paralysis
Clot in bowel vein
Inflammation of bowel lining
Blood clot in left thigh

All this: and still the fight goes on

In some ways euthanasia seems like another compassionate act, if it is requested. But, say the objectors, would the recognition of euthanasia by the law lead to a kind of free-for-all, where nobody who wasn't 'useful' was allowed to survive? After all, mass extermination of the old and the mentally or physically handicapped took place in Nazi concentration camps. Is there a possibility that euthanasia seems a good idea because it removes another of those nasty things we don't like to face: a suffering death? Or would you like to have the last word about your own body?

There are areas in which men have control over their own death; it doesn't take them by surprise. Differences in attitude to these exist not only in our own culture, but in cultures throughout the world. For us, the suicide is an unhappy man who cannot find comfort in living. Yet the Greek or Roman suicide might be a warrior about to be defeated on the battlefield or in politics. His death would avoid the defeat and disgrace, and salvage his honour through the courage with which he met it. The kami-kaze pilots of Japan guided their one-man planes, packed with explosive, into enemy targets. Paradise was the reward for this service to the Emperor, according to their religion. In other places people have killed themselves when they were ecstatically happy. Hindu widows were expected, perhaps compelled, to burn themselves to death when their husbands

died. (Husbands weren't obliged to return the favour when their wives died!)

It all seems very strange from our point of view. But think how recently *that* has changed. Not long ago the suicide of a German army officer was reported. He had been involved in exercises in which several soldiers were killed, perhaps through his error. But the authorities announced that his suicide was not connected with this disgrace, but with 'domestic difficulties'. This is what we expect a modern suicide to be. Would a Roman-style suicide of honour help the reputation of a disgraced soldier or statesman these days?

Though the very idea of public execution nowadays fills most of us with horror, there are public executions going on throughout the world. A Ghanaian newspaper carried a photograph of some small boys sitting on a fence, with the caption 'Part of the happy crowd at yesterday's public execution. . .'. And the offence which merits this punishment can seem strange to us. In the Ukraine a factory manager is shot for falsifying the accounts, and in many countries, thieves are executed. Attitudes like these give underlying clues to the most important beliefs and principles in a society.

Crowds queue to see desert murderer hang

THERE WERE traffic jams in Kuwait at 8 a.m. last Wednesday as thousands of car owners (few walk in Kuwait) rushed to get a grandstand view of a 34-year-old Syrian, Abdul Karim Alzamel, being hanged in the walled compound of the Naif palace,

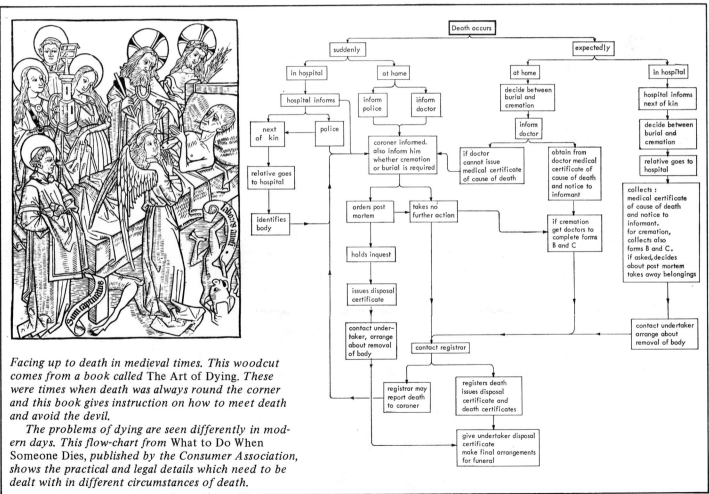

Facing up to death in medieval times. This woodcut comes from a book called The Art of Dying. *These were times when death was always round the corner and this book gives instruction on how to meet death and avoid the devil.*

The problems of dying are seen differently in modern days. This flow-chart from What to Do When Someone Dies, *published by the Consumer Association, shows the practical and legal details which need to be dealt with in different circumstances of death.*

What does DEATH look like?

Most people haven't seen a corpse. Why should they want to? Well, there's just plain curiosity, to begin with.

'The youth looked keenly at the ashen face. The wind raised the tawny beard. It moved as if a hand were stroking it. He vaguely desired to walk around the body and stare; the impulse of the living to try to read in dead eyes the answer to the Question.'

Stephen Crane
The Red Badge of Courage

People know before they start that the answer isn't there, but they still have a desire to look. And they are rather nervous of what they will see:

'When I began nursing I realised that I was going to see death at close quarters. I hadn't before, and I was petrified. I was afraid of seeing a dead body, not of seeing someone dying. We'd been working for a few weeks and someone died on one of the wards. A girl in our set had helped to prepare the body. At lunch-time we were all on to her: "What did he look like? What happened?" It was as though it would help us over it when we saw it ourselves. Now I know that, at

first, anyway, a person doesn't change when they die; they usually look much better, especially if they've suffered. Their faces are relaxed and you do get a sense of relief. When somebody is dead you imagine they'll seem changed, and that's frightening. Once I'd seen a dead body I knew I would never be frightened again.'

A nurse

Even a medical dictionary, with its stark list of things to look for in a corpse, doesn't make the appearance of death sound very frightening:

'Death, signs of: Relaxing of facial muscles, producing rather staring eyes and gaping mouth. Loss of curves of the back, which becomes flat against the bed or table. Slight discolouration of the skin, which becomes a wax-yellow hue,

The grandmother of King Baudouin of Belgium died aged eighty-nine.

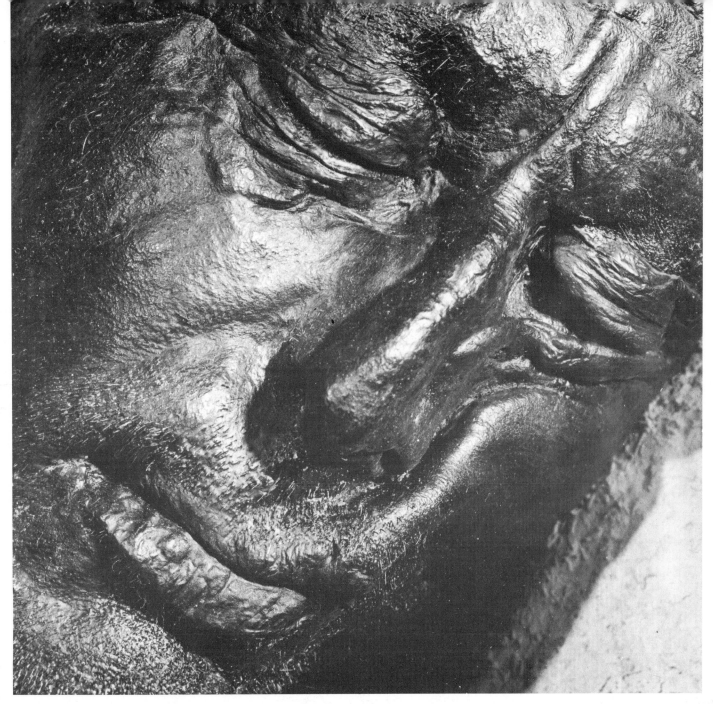

The Tollund Man died two thousand years ago. His head has been preserved by the tannic acid in the peat bog where he was buried.

and loses its pink transparency at the finger-webs.

The only certain sign of death, however, is stoppage of the heart, and to ensure that this is permanent, it is necessary to listen over the heart, that is, over the chest at the inner side of the nipple, for five minutes. This can be done by means of a stethoscope or by listening directly with the ear on the chest.

Stoppage of breathing should also be noted, and this can be confirmed by observing that a mirror held before the mouth shows no haze.'

Black's Medical Dictionary

It's all rather simple and old-fashioned, isn't it? The immediate effect of death is clearly not all that startling. The corpse changes *gradually*. At first it looks just like life, then less and less so. Dr. Lyall Watson, in *The Romeo Error* has suggested that, since human beings are dying from the moment they are born (and even before then, if you consider that a foetus is covered with hair which falls off before birth) then the moment of death is just an advanced stage of what we are experiencing all the time as we live. Certainly the appearance of a corpse immediately after death is enough like life for it to be treated, at first, as it was when alive:

'After death we wash the corpse, comb the hair, try to make them look as nice as we can. When you're washing a corpse you often expect it to move. It may be a bit cold, but when you turn it over, you somehow expect the muscles to respond. You put an arm through a night-dress and you expect a helping push. For the first few hours after death most dead bodies look more or less asleep, certainly not horrific.

Once the corpse has been laid out, it is taken from the ward as soon as possible because there's no point, really, in keeping them on the ward. On some wards there's a patient waiting in casualty to get into the bed. When somebody dies on the ward, you screen everybody off while that patient is taken out, even though they know he's dead. Knowing it and seeing it are different things.'

A nurse

As you may have read in detective stories, it is possible to tell from the state of the body, the time that has passed since death occurred. There are four ways of doing this: after the body has been dead for three hours, marks like bruises appear on the back. The blood is running into the lowest part of the body, obeying the laws of gravity, as one might expect. If the body is lying face downwards, then obviously the marks will appear on the front. Immediately after death the body starts to cool, and after twelve hours it has become as cold as the surrounding air. But the surrounding air may not be all that cold, of course, so the 'icy hand' of death is not really accurate, especially in these days of central heating.

After six hours 'rigor mortis' begins, takes about six hours to spread through the body, remains for twelve hours and passes off during the next twelve. Again, it is a gradual process, it can vary according to the things the person was doing before

they died. It is sometimes thought that a corpse immediately becomes stiff and hard, so that it's necessary to stretch it out nice and straight as soon as you can, otherwise it'll never go in the coffin.

Putrefaction, or rotting, usually begins after two or three days, as a greenish colour on the stomach. From looking more or less like a living person, the corpse changes. It begins to fall to pieces, or decompose. This is the most unpleasant bit, but it doesn't begin right away, and usually, before it sets in properly, the corpse has been disposed of, so that people are not offended by it.

This gradual nature of decomposition means that it is possible, in European countries, to keep the corpse at home before the funeral, though this is now unusual in Britain. In fact, it seems that only very rich people, who have spare rooms, or poor people, who keep traditional practices longer, have the corpse in the house. The majority have it kept in the undertaker's shop in a 'chapel of rest', where they can visit it if they wish. Usually only the closest relatives do so. Perhaps this is a better arrangement than keeping a corpse at home. It is certainly more convenient. But it seems that the gradual onset of the appearances of death is tailor-made to help mourners come to terms with their loss. Unpleasant though it sounds to those who have not seen a corpse, to be with the dead body before it is disposed of, is to have an opportunity to accept the death and make farewells. We deprive ourselves of this opportunity by resigning our dead to the 'chapel of rest'.

Skeleton in the cupboard ?

A 17th Century picture shows Londoners fleeing the city beset by plague. But they are pursued by the plague-death in the figure of a skeleton.

Right: *In earlier times people lived more closely with the idea of death. The dance of death was a common theme.*

The death theme in the contemporary world?—in the form of a plastic car ornament.

Right: *Coming to terms with death: a Papuan from New Guinea uses his grandmother's skull as a pillow. Her spirit protects him as he sleeps.*

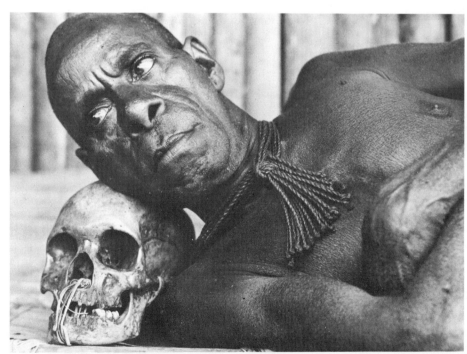

MOURNING

Once a death has happened it is the people left behind who have the problems. When somebody you care for is alive, it is very difficult to imagine what your life would be like without them. Somebody is there, then they are absent, and they will never come back. It is not surprising that the first reaction to a death is usually to disbelieve it. The certainty lingers that your person will walk through the door. . . The closer you were to them, the more this certainty persists. Time is supposed to heal in these circumstances, and as it passes this initial, optimistic feeling goes with it, leaving many mixed reactions. The need for the bereaved to be alone and quiet, conflicts with the need to talk at length about the death:

'what happened immediately before, and what happened afterwards, and what they did on that day, and how they wish they had done something else, and what the nurse said. Then they often want to talk about the person who has died, and their relationship with them. And they want to say it over and over again'.

It's clear that those in mourning need listeners to whom they can do all this talking. The lady speaking above is a volunteer, who visits people who have been bereaved, mainly just to listen.

Next there is the angry, resentful feeling. It is a feeling that occurs at other times, too. The whole world is going on as usual, and this disaster has happened. We feel affronted by the normality of other peoples' lives, we resent them. And yet we need their support and company. Maybe these contradictory attitudes in those who are bereaved is one of the reasons why they are avoided. And they can be embarrassing, they might burst into tears; and boring, going over and over the same story — and *they* might well be *us*. There is no way to prepare yourself for bereavement unless it is to try to understand and listen when

'You can't rely on professional mourners like you used to . . . '

28

somebody who is bereaved needs your company.

People who are bereaved actually change physically. They lose weight, they don't sleep very well. Doctors prescribe drugs to help them sleep and perhaps to keep them in a state of respectable non-indulgence in violent grief. But still they dream of the dead person and sometimes they have vivid experiences that he or she is close to them. These experiences seem to be comforting. During the six months after the death of a husband or wife, there is a far higher chance that the surviving partner will die. A bereavement is obviously an enormous blow, an enormous change. Yet at the present time it is the British custom to continue almost as if nothing had happened. Looking round about, can you see any-one in mourning? Without a doubt some-body *is* in mourning. But outward and visible signs in dress or behaviour are not shown. Carrying on as normal means that few people change their social lives, or even draw the curtains of their house.

*Royal mourners at the funeral of **King Gustav of Sweden**.*

Peace perfect Peace.

In Memoriam.

Grief

A woodcut by Käthe Kollwitz.

A funeral procession in Ghana.

A cemetery in Vietnam.

Grief for a leader in India.

Tragedy in Cyprus

31

'And a good thing too,' a funeral director told me. 'People have got far more modern about mourning.' But is outwardly treating a death as little more than a minor inconvenience really a good thing? The indications are that human beings need to mourn openly, to mark this enormous change, and that if they do not do so they will suffer mentally.

The Victorians went a bit far perhaps with their mourning. Clothes were swathed in a dull black cloth called crape, on the sale of which many modern textile firms built their fortunes. Widows spent two years in full mourning, all their clothes covered in this crape. After two years, half-mourning could be worn: grey, lavender, mauve and violet. With the clothes went a ban on all socializing: the widow visited no friend for twelve months. Children all wore mourning too, and the household servants. There were regulation periods of mourning for relatives of differing nearness, and one was particularly odd: 'complimentary mourning'. A man's second wife (there were many second wives because large numbers of women died in childbirth) must wear slight mourning for three months for the death of his first wife's parents, or two months for his first wife's brothers and sisters.

Queen Victoria's own grief and mourning are famous. After the death of her husband, Prince Albert, she had his rooms and possessions kept as he had left them, and every day his clothes were laid out and his shaving water brought. It is as though she got stuck in the first, disbelieving stage of grief. This is found nowadays:

'The house is just as it was, even the dog lead; he always kept it there, and the dog used to get it to go out for a walk at night; his pipe is still over there, his glasses and his hearing aid and his tobacco. My brother-in-law wanted me to clear all his clothes out, but I couldn't.'

A widow

'Two llamas, called Charlie and Josephine, were inseparable companions for 13 years. They escaped from their pen in a snowstorm and Charlie, who after his escape, was 'unmanageable' was precipitately shot by police. Josephine, who was standing nearby then slowly approached Charlie and sank to her knees. She rested her head silently on his bloody body and refused to move. She appeared to witnesses to be suffering from overwhelming grief. Josephine died 15 minutes later. Her keeper said that her health was absolutely normal the day before.'

Sunday Times

Animals get their memorials too. This is a large animal cemetery in East London.

There are many clues to the feelings and progress of grief in the Death Announcements and In Memoriam sections of newspapers, both national and local. It is interesting to compare the style of a serious national paper, and the sort of people whose deaths appear in it, with your local paper. You can find out how long after the death families continue to insert In Memoriam notices; which family relationships are most often remembered. Small pieces of poetry are sometimes used. Are these written by the mourners, or chosen from a selection that the local paper offers them? If you are interested, you might ask someone on your local paper how they organise this part of the job.

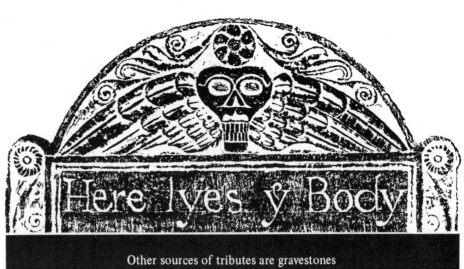

Here lyes ye Body

Other sources of tributes are gravestones and plaques in churches, and the words on these are known as epitaphs.

'Mine eyes wax heavy, and the days grow cold.
Draw, draw the closed curtains and make room:
My dear, my dearest dust; I come, I come.'

Lady Catherine Dyer's epitaph
on her husband's monument

'One year has passed since that sad day,
You closed your eyes and passed away,
As each day dawns and starts anew,
We never fail to think of you.'

from a local newspaper

'Here lies in peace a Hampshire Grenadier
Who caught his death by drinking cold, small beer.'

from a soldier's tomb

'John Bird, a labourer, lies here,
Who served the earth for thirty year
With spade and mattock, drill and plough;
But never found it kind till now.'

Sylvia Townsend Warner

In Memoriam

BURNAGE, Stan. — In loving memory of dad, November 15, 1974. — Nuala, John and grandsons. 4

BURNAGE, Stanley. — Sadly missed but not forgotten.
—Shean, Margaret and Nicholas. 4

CREASEY. — In loving memory of our dear Mum who fell asleep on November 21, 1973.
A prayer and a thought are all we can give,
But we'll never forget you as long as we live,
Helpful, thoughtful, willing and kind,
We are proud of the memory you left behind.
—God bless. Still sadly missed by Lily, Ernie, George, Leslie and families. P4

SHINE, Elizabeth. — Passed away November 11, 1973.
To Mum,
A light is from our household gone,
A voice we loved is stilled,
A place is vacant in our hearts, Which never can be filled.
—Rose, Bill and children.

The funeral home

Funeral homes are a relatively new development in Britain. Based on an American idea, they offer a new style of luxury and convenience in dealing with the dead. They take responsibility for the whole funeral procedure from the time of death to the actual burial or cremation. This one which serves the whole of the South Wales area is open to 'clients' 7 days a week, 24 hours a day. In the words of its Director, 'a funeral home takes the place of the actual residence where the deceased lived, and takes the strain off the residents or relatives living there'.

The rooms in which the dead are displayed have elaborate decoration in contrast to the starkness of the refrigerated area in which the bodies are stored at first. A mortician who works at Roath Court was fully in favour of this kind of funeral arrangement: 'I think these rest rooms are wonderful; much better than having the body at home. Very few places are really suited to having a body lying at home — you don't want the cat walking all over it. The rest room softens the whole thing'.

This funeral home employs a number of people to do jobs associated with the business, such as managing the flowers. When they recruited workers to trim and finish the coffins the advertisement made no mention of the nature of the work, stating simply 'ladies required for interesting furnishing work'.

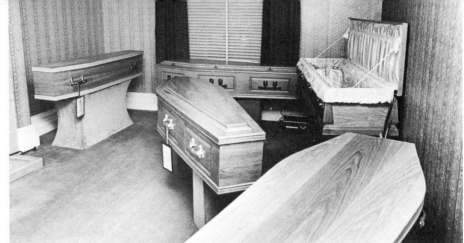

The funeral home makes it a rule that relatives of the bereaved come to view the body – just in case a mistake of identity has been made.

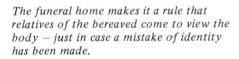

Before they are laid out in the rest rooms, the corpses are stored in refrigerated conditions. Preparing the bodies for view is seen as an important part of the job. 'You get them in all conditions, and clean them up so that they're nice to look at. It makes it much softer for the relatives to see them looking nice and rested.'

Ritual

'Do you have to spend your days off whistling solemn music?'

The British cremation is a sign of the gradual disappearance of ritual in the disposing of the dead. It is quick and clean, and when it is over everybody goes back to work. In some homes the funeral meal, the 'baked meats', are still something of a ritual, and those at the funeral go back together to eat and begin their relationships with one another and without the dead person. But on the whole there isn't much left of the patterns of celebration which are strong and important elements in most cultures. To celebrate any event according to an old pattern, followed by generations of people, can give those taking part a feeling of history, and inspire them with awe. But some people have neither feelings of awe nor history when they take part in ritual events, and find them, on the contrary, rather an empty and unspontaneous way of marking an occasion.

In fact, most societies have made a fuss of some sort about the important events in an individual's life. The front runners for this treatment are birth, marriage and death. In cultures which have been dominated for a long time by the Christian church, the rituals have become absorbed into church ceremonial. But initiation, marriage and funeral are celebrated by people who aren't Christian, and were celebrated long before Christianity. The *need* for ritual has always been there, which makes it strange that the 'rites of passage' of most Britons have become subdued almost to vanishing point.

Why has this happened? The opponents of ritual point to all sorts of horrors carried out in its name. It seems that, in times of threat and tension, what is a necessary and helpful part of a culture, giving people strength and a sense of community, is used as a demonstration of strength against outsiders. The Orange Marches, a community focus and a commemorative ritual for Protestants in Northern Ireland, have become an assertive and aggressive display. And the IRA funeral extends beyond the real intention.

Perhaps you think that you don't want a fuss made about your corpse anyway? That it's daft to spend a lot of money on someone who can't enjoy it? A newspaper stopped people at random on the street and asked what they wanted for their funerals:

'A very cheap one. . . '

'Just a plain Catholic Service.'

'I would like a quiet funeral.'

'I don't care for pomp and circumstance.'

'They can heave me in the Bay and feed the fishes for all I care.'

'As long as they make sure I'm dead I don't care what they do next.'

The trouble is, as we've seen already, it is the people left behind who have the problems, and it was to give them support that rituals evolved. Would they prefer to dispose of their dead with a bit more pomp and circumstance than they get these days?

The ritual of death in Ghana.

The body of Cardinal Heenan lying in state in the Roman Catholic Cathedral at Westminster. Watching over the body before it is buried is a survival of the feeling that we need to make sure that it really is dead.

Funeral procession in Turkey.

Right: *An elaborate Italian funeral carriage.*

A black limousine for the final journey in a British street.

I will teach you my townspeople
how to perform a funeral
for you have it over a troop
of artists —
unless one should scour the world —
you have the ground sense necessary.

See! the hearse leads.
I begin with a design for a hearse.
For Christ's sake not black —
nor white either — and not polished!
Let it be weathered — like a farm
   wagon —
with gilt wheels (this could be
applied fresh at small expense)
or no wheels at all:
a rough dray to drag over the ground.

Knock the glass out!
My God — glass, my townspeople!
For what purpose? is it for the dead
to look out or for us to see
how well he is housed or to see
the flowers or the lack of them —
or what?
To keep the rain and snow from him?
He will have a heavier rain soon:
pebbles and dirt and what not.

Let there be no glass —
and no upholstery, phew!
and no little brass rollers
and small easy wheels on the bottom —
my townspeople what are you
   thinking of?
A rough plain hearse then
with gilt wheels and no top at all.
On this the coffin lies
by its own weight.

   No wreaths please —
especially no hot-house flowers.
Some common memento is better,
something he prized and is known by:
his old clothes — a few books
   perhaps —
God knows what! You realize
how we are about these things
my townspeople —
something will be found — anything
even flowers if he had come to that.
So much for the hearse.

For heaven's sake, though, see to the
   driver!
Take off the silk hat! In fact

that's no place at all for him —
up there unceremoniously
dragging our friend out to his own
   dignity!
Bring him down — bring him down!
Low and inconspicuous! I'd not have
   him ride
on the wagon at all — damn him —
the undertaker's understrapper!
Let him hold the reins
and walk at the side
and inconspicuously too!

   Then briefly as to yourselves:
Walk behind — as they do in France,
seventh class, or if you do ride
Hell take curtains! Go with some show
of inconvenience; sit openly —
to the weather as to grief.
Or do you think you can shut grief in?
What — from us? We who have perhaps
nothing to lose? Share with us
share with us — it will be money
in your pockets.
        Go now
I think you are ready.

William Carlos Williams

Mechanization is taking over in the graveyard. It means less backbreaking work for the grave-digger but other problems are created for him by a multi-racial society with different burial customs.

The reluctant gravediggers

THE National Front is exploiting a delicate situation in Blackburn, where the town's four gravediggers are refusing to prepare cemetery plots for the burial of Muslims whose families want them interred in traditional Islamic fashion, in shrouds rather than coffins.

The Front has expressed its support for the gravediggers, who did not solicit it, and it is trying to spread the boycott to other Lancashire towns with Muslim communities.

The gravediggers say they object to the smell of rapidly decomposing bodies buried without coffins, which affects them when they are digging new graves in neighbouring plots, and which, they have been told, may be a health hazard.

They object also to the demands of Muslims for wider graves than those customary in this country and the threat to their five-day week because some Muslim families insist on burials at only 24 hours' notice.

'I appreciate it's more efficient but I still feel it's lacking in respect.'

41

The ritual is, or ought to be, a pattern of behaviour by which people can conduct themselves even when they can hardly think about their own behaviour, and by which those around them can conduct themselves. In a ritual you know what to do. Some countries have a funeral ritual which incorporates violent exhibition of grief. In the Middle East mourners tear their hair and claw at their own skins, abandoning themselves to misery. Even those who are not closely involved share in this demonstration. In many countries alcohol is an important part of the funeral celebration. To see crowds of mourners, drunk and dancing at an African funeral, can be a shocking experience for someone reared on the subdued, undemonstrative British variety. Isn't it rather disrespectful to prance about drunk at a funeral? Or is it just an honest way to drown your sorrows?

One essential ingredient of ritual is participation. Yet as we have handed over our dying to the medical profession, we have surrendered our dead to the under-takers. In the old days, family and friends organised the funeral, while a priest said the prayers. The priest is still there but a professional arranges all the other details and the family and friends just watch. It is rare for a funeral to be carried out without the services of an undertaker, and it is easy to see why. Shattered by the death, the closest relatives are relieved to hand over troublesome arrangements to a quietly spoken and competent arranger. And because funeral directors are there, the role of friends and community in arranging the funeral is no longer necessary. So the old-style funeral dis-

TIME GENTS FOR THE FUNERAL OF THE GUVNOR

HALF an hour before closing, a hush fell over The Vine public house The locals drained their glasses. It was Time—for the landlord's funeral.

His coffin stood on trestles in the corner. The Rev Reginald Parsons, the Methodist Minister at Cradley, near Halesowen, Worcs, conducted the service in the public bar. And more than 100 regulars crowded in to pay their last respects.

They were remembering the last wish of landlord Harold Garratt, who died at the age of 63.

The service began at about the time Harold would have hung a towel over the pumps.

appears and it's difficult to remember which came first, the funeral or the funeral director.

'I asked whether in England it would be possible for a survivor to by-pass the funeral establishment altogether and take the deceased directly to the crematorium. Such a thing did happen once in Mr Ashton's experience. Two young men drove up in a Bedford van and said they wanted to buy a coffin. Mr Ashton told them he didn't sell coffins, he sold funerals. The young men insisted that they did not wish a funeral; their mother had died, they had procured a properly issued death certificate, they had been out to Enfield crematorium to make all the arrangements, they intended to buy a coffin and take their mother out there themselves. "We chatted and chatted", Mr Ashton recalled. "Finally I was convinced they were on the level, so I sold them a coffin. What could I do? They weren't doing anything wrong, there

was nothing to stop them. But it really shook me. Afterwards I rang up the chap at the crematorium and said: Did that shake you? It shook *me*".'

Jessica Mitford
The American Way of Death

Remember that this is the funeral *business*. Funerals can be bigger or smaller, more or less elaborate, and they cost accordingly. The cost is usually related to the sort of coffin chosen, the more expensive coffin getting the more elaborate funeral. There is a range of price, from £70 to more than £120, and these prices often don't cover all the 'extras', like the embalming, or the shroud. Obviously these are not details that the recently bereaved want to argue about. But buying a funeral should be treated in as business-like a way as the purchase of any expensive item. On the whole, funeral directors see themselves as part of a service industry, and act with a good deal of care and consideration. But are there thoughts like *this* in the back of their minds?

'It seems highly probable that the most satisfactory funeral service for the average family is one in which the cost has necessitated some degree of sacrifice. This permits the survivors to atone for any real or fancied neglect of the deceased prior to his death.'

from the *National Funeral Service Journal of America*

Many funeral businesses grew from the supply of coffins by carpenters, or of carriages by stables, or of burial clothes and mourning. This last is the trade on which some large department stores were founded, and you will often find they have a discreet funeral 'service'. Many firms are still family concerns, and these recruit more easily into what sounds just about the gloomiest job in the world. Who would become an undertaker and why?

'I was apprenticed to a cabinet maker. When the war came in 1939 our work was limited and we had to turn to coffin-making or go out of business. We used to deliver these coffins to the undertaker, and he and I got talking one day about the work. I'd become interested in embalming after reading a book about the Egyptians, so when he offered me a job I said I'd like to learn embalming. I was earning 32/- a week and he offered me £2/5/-. It didn't take too long to decide.'
An undertaker

Another undertaker takes a different view:

'An undertaker's job is round the clock. We are always on call, and we provide a service. We deal one third with the deceased and two thirds with the bereaved — folk who are living, shocked, don't know where to turn. I wouldn't do the job if it weren't for the help I feel I'm giving.'

And here's yet another undertaker:

'One thing I'll predict: funerals are going to get more expensive. It is an underpaid industry, and in the past 15—20 years it hasn't been attracting young people. This is an awful job. If you want somebody to do it, you've got to pay them really well. We think nothing of paying a professional accountant £5000 a year. You'd never notice if he wasn't there. But you'd soon notice if the undertakers stopped work.'

The final act. A minister reads the last words of the funeral service as the coffin is lowered into the grave.

Clocking on.

All in a day's work

'I don't know any other occupation that is carried as much from father to son as funeral direction, nobody else would do it. I've never met anybody who'd offer to change jobs with me.' A Funeral Director

The business of the undertaker is usually shrouded in sombre mystery. These photographs, specially taken for this book, show what goes on during a day in a family firm of undertakers.

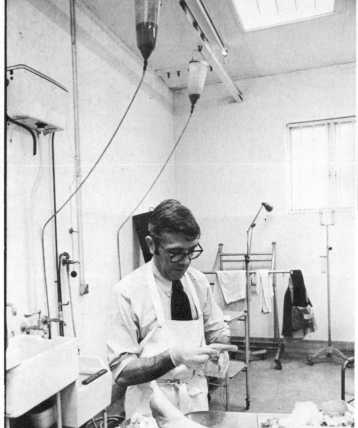

In the workshop.

Furnishing the coffin.

In the lab — where embalming takes place.

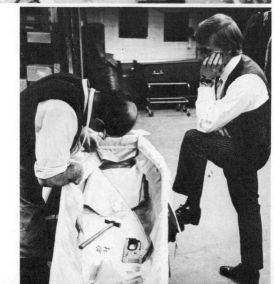

The Director describes the kind of social function that undertakers have: 'Death has no respect of time, place or person. It is nothing to receive a call at two o'clock in the morning, and somebody will say, "My mother has died. I'm living all alone here, what do I do?" Now at that time of day, there is nothing we can do for that dear lady but listen to what she has to say . . .'

The finishing touch.

At the wheel.

Loading up – a respectful ritual.

This Director also described some of the effects of grief. 'Grief is something like an iceberg. A little bit points out of the water and two-thirds is hidden underneath. Some people at the time of death can show only a very small part of grief. There are varying reasons. It could be that it's a man, and maybe he feels his position as the man in the house is to uphold tradition and be manly. It may be that a person is just not used to communicating in which case you just have to wait for things to happen.'

After DEATH

I wonder if the things that happen after death are particularly nasty to consider because we, warm and living people, imagine them happening to us as we are now? Burial or burning are ghastly prospects, decomposition a horrific thought, in terms of living flesh. (Perhaps this is one of the reasons why young death seems inappropriate.) But if you disassociate yourself from the whole business, and consider it against the natural world, it doesn't seem half so bad. The decaying of a human body is the same rotting process as the decaying of leaves in winter time. This over-used comparison does not make the actuality of human decomposition any pleasanter. But it is a fact that decomposition is not confined to human dead; all animal and vegetable matter rots in the same way. There isn't much point in keeping this dead thing around. It has no use, it doesn't look or smell very good, and it takes up space.

If natural decomposition at its quickest is required, then the body should go straight into the ground, perhaps in a shroud, as in Israel. But the course of nature isn't acceptable to everybody, and in some societies there has been an attempt to combat it by preserving the dead. The Egyptian mummy is a famous example from ancient times, but this was exceptional; it was far more common to assist the natural breakdown of the corpse by burning or burying it.

In the eighteenth century, an English doctor devised a process for draining blood from the dead body and replacing it with preserving fluid. This treatment was not practised by the general public, but it was used for kings and leaders. There was a practical reason for embalming these people. We have already seen that the death of leaders is often disbelieved. After all, they are not just men, but men in whom power is vested. So it is important to establish that they *are* dead, and to prove that they died naturally, or at least, in the way it is *said* they died.

Alexander the Great was preserved in wax and honey. Lord Nelson's body was brought back from the Battle of Trafalgar in a barrel of brandy. President Peron of Argentina owed much of his popularity to his wife Eva, and when she died he had

Embalming – making the corpse 'sweet'. The internal organs are drained of blood and injected with embalming fluid.

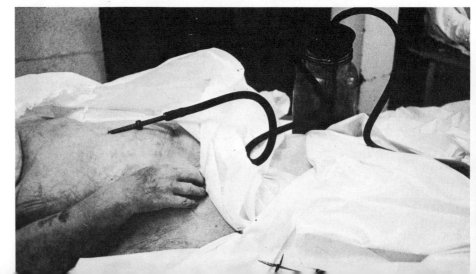

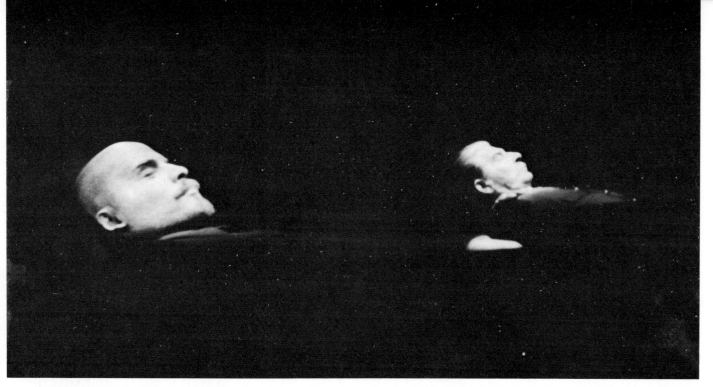

The embalmed bodies of Lenin and Stalin in the Moscow Mausoleum. Lenin died in 1924, Stalin in 1953.

her embalmed corpse displayed in Buenos Aires in a glass coffin. When he was deposed, the corpse came with him to Europe. Eventually he again became President of Argentina and back he went, with his new wife – and Eva. In Moscow the corpse of Lenin receives a constant stream of visitors in the Kremlin mausoleum.

It is now quite usual in Britain for corpses to be embalmed. Funeral directors, who supervise nearly every disposal these days, claim that this is more 'hygienic'. As far as I can gather, there is no medical evidence to prove that embalming prevents diseases being spread by corpses, or even that diseases *are* spread by corpses.

It is a very vague area, about which facts are hard to come by. It is possible to see the funeral director's point of view when he says that it makes his own work a good deal easier if a corpse is first embalmed. The Consumer's Association quote a charge of between £3 and £8 for this service, which is probably fair enough, even if it is only for the benefit of the undertaker. Of course, if bodies were buried by their families, and this were done within three days of death, embalming wouldn't be necessary and the money would be saved.

In the United States, embalming of corpses has become an important contribution to funeral ceremonial. Coffins

there are open at the funeral, and it is a 'cosmetician' who gets to work on the face of the corpse, to make it look like life, or better, if possible:

'The patching and filling (by the embalmer) completed, "Mr. Jones" is now shaved, washed, and dressed. Cream-based cosmetic, available in pink, flesh and suntan, brunette and blonde, is applied to his hands and face, his hair is shampooed and combed (and, in the case of Mrs. Jones, set), his hands are manicured. For the horny-handed son of toil, special care must be taken. Cream should be applied to remove ingrained grime, and the nails cleaned.'

Jessica Mitford *The American Way of Death*

American embalmers and cosmeticians can repair severe mutilation — and even decapitation. But their preserving methods are designed to improve the immediate appearance of the corpse rather than to stave off decomposition for long. The type of embalming designed to prevent decomposition is liable to make the corpse look worse than life, not better. With most modern embalming decomposition soon sets in after the corpse is buried. Perhaps the implication that an embalmed corpse, looking 'nicer than life' will retain this state is a rather dishonest one. One dissatisfied American customer actually had his mother's body exhumed and then sued the funeral director when it was found to have rotted most unpleasantly. In fact, the decomposition of an embalmed corpse is far more unpleasant than natural decomposition. Moulds, the sort that grow on stale bread, quickly decorate it, creating a monster from the cosmetician's work of art. But funeral directors claim that as well as the hygienic necessity for embalming, it is helpful for mourners to see the corpse 'at its best' before disposal. It is also a practice in America to use the strongest, nature-proof coffins, and to enclose these in concrete or heavy metal 'vaults', which are linings to the grave. The aim seems to be to beat the natural order as far as possible. Does this tell us anything about modern American society? Needless to say, it all adds considerably to the actual cost of the funeral.

In other societies the need to dispose of the dead, rather than to preserve them, has been heightened by fear of 'spirits'.

'The Tasmanians tied bodies to prevent them from moving. In Australia the hollow tree which serves as a coffin may be pierced with a spear to nail the neck of the departed to his prison, or the whole tree may be set on fire after the burial. The nailing of the dead to wooden boards in their graves developed into a regular funeral rite in prehistoric Spain. Whole cemeteries have been found where the skeletons showed all the evidences of a second killing by the piercing of their skulls with huge nails.'

Julius Lips *The Origin of Things*

What a contrast with modern America!

Vegetable and animal decay are part of a cycle in which decomposition is essential to birth and growth. The decaying body breaks down into simple elements, which, if it is buried, are already contained in the earth. These elements are being constantly replaced as a source of new life: a compost heap is essential for a garden which is expected to grow things year after year.

But burial is no longer always practical, though it has a strong traditional hold in rural communities. Those churchyards in villages and country towns, with their grassy mounds, lichen-encrusted tombstones and a wealth of wild flowers — what peaceful and interesting places! 'Who could imagine unquiet slumbers for the sleepers in that quiet earth?' But nowadays even small villages have extended the churchyard to the less charming field across the road and, if you are a town dweller, your own chances of burial will be in a cemetery.

Cemeteries began as highly profitable Victorian ventures. In one of the first cemeteries the sale of graves was at £1700 per acre. Since it was expensive, burial in cemeteries was thought rather smart, in the strange way that fashions grow. They were called 'necropoli' and famous architects designed and built them. Now every local authority has a rather unprepossessing acreage, jam-packed with memorials, and if you hope to be buried, that's where you'll end up.

This enterprising cemetery in London welcomes visitors as individuals, and in parties, to its 'Tombstone Trail'. Its leaflet describes the flora and wildlife as well as some of the famous memorials and gravestones.

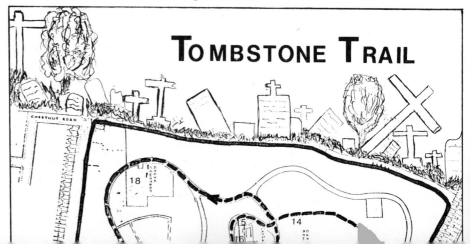

VICTORIAN cemeteries, their monuments, and family vaults romantically overgrown, and crumbling, are increasingly becoming the scene of midnight witchcraft sex orgies, a senior Scotland Yard detective said yesterday.

Desecration of tombs by witchcraft fanatics was becoming "a national problem" in places as far afield as Devon and Lancashire, as well as the Gothic Victoriana of Highgate Cemetery.

They really are ugly places. In the past 50 years by-laws have been introduced governing the sort of tombstones that can be erected in cemeteries, and these have meant that there is not much room for individual taste and imagination. The result is a bunch of boring slabs, just sufficiently out of alignment to be a shambles, not enough to be charming. . .

'The latest and flattest development is the Lawn Cemetery. . . The stones are now abolished completely, and only a small, bronze tablet, flush in the grass, is allowed, so that the motor-mower can go straight over it; a great advance on the previous childishly simple and economical method of keeping church-yards trim by pasturing sheep in them, so that the grass was cropped in one, almost silent, operation.'

Barbara Jones *Design for Death*

As far as I can gather, it is possible to bury a corpse almost anywhere, providing the private burial is registered. However, where you do it depends on who owns the freehold of the land, and whether the use of the land is restricted in the deeds. In theory, then, you could be buried in your own back garden, if the deeds of your house allow . . . except that you must first obtain planning permission and get approval from the Department of the Environment. And then your neighbours can object and . . . it would all take far too long, of course. Which is why you don't find many people being buried in back gardens. It wouldn't help when the house came to be sold, either.

The thought of burial alive is a nightmare which makes some people determined not to be buried. In the last century Count Karnice-Karnicki had a nasty experience at the funeral of a young Belgian girl. As the earth fell on the lid of her coffin, it woke her from a trance or coma which had been taken for death. Her screams upset the Count, and, horrified by the situation, he decided to invent some way of preventing these tragedies. In the end he came up with a hermetically-sealed coffin with a long tube, about 13 centimetres in diameter, fixed in the lid above the breast of the corpse. There was a glass ball here, connected to a spring which ran up the tube into a box, which would be 'at the surface' as it were. The slightest movement of the chest would move the glass ball, the spring would be released, and the lid of the box would fly open, letting light and air into the coffin. At the same time a flag would unfurl, a bell ring for half an hour, a lamp burn after dark, and the tube would magnify the yells of the 'corpse'. All this for an estimated 13 shillings. Daft as it sounds, this story makes sense to people who find burial frightening to contemplate. But strict laws about the examination of corpses by a doctor seem to have made it unlikely that anybody will need to invent more extraordinary machinery to prevent being buried alive.

But in all probability there won't be any earth burial of the dead, either, quite soon. Currently 144 new acres of land are taken up every year by burials.

The cremation of Dr. William Price in 1875. He was among the first to advocate cremation but there was much opposition to this practice.

A German undertaker offers a popular service — scattering the ashes of the dead at sea. He has found that this appeals to land-dwellers rather than sailors and to women more than men.

The traditional funeral pyres on the banks of the Ganges. Do-it-yourself cremation is ruled out in Britain by legal requirements.

More and more corpses are being disposed of by another old method which also, in the end, means that the decaying organic material is placed back in the natural cycle. This is burning, which sounds a bit brutal, and is usually called cremation. It was practiced by ancient societies, especially in the East, but it is quite new to Britain. There were only three cremations in 1885. Now the majority of corpses are burned.

This is done in a crematorium, and one crematorium serves a much larger area than a cemetery. It is a highly mechanised establishment, fronted by chapels, where a short service is conducted before the coffin disappears discreetly behind a curtain or doors, to be trundled off to an incinerator. Most crematoria still look very new, and many mourners are rather shocked by the atmosphere of places which sometimes deal with forty-five corpses a day. It is distinctly conveyer-belt. Since the crematoria serve large

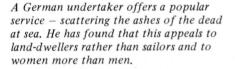

areas, the brief service in the chapel will generally be said by a clergyman who had no personal knowledge of the dead person. After cremation the ashes are removed from the incinerator and scattered, usually in a flower garden of remembrance. Sometimes a rose tree is planted, or a small plaque with the name of the dead person is erected. These are generally removed after several years.

Although the practice of burning is clearly sensible, it seems to be contributing to the general playing-down of death in Britain today. The crematorium is not much imbued with the sense of occasion that even a small church can give, and the feeling that your particular corpse was important gets rather lost when you are queuing up to wait your turn in the chapel. The funeral pyre of other countries gives burning a significance and impressiveness that we miss. But could we permit funeral pyres in back gardens and in smokeless zones?

'Until 1965 it was illegal to cremate the body of anyone who had left instructions that he did not wish it. Now, however, there is no such restriction, and executors or next of kin are free to cremate or not, as they choose. Even if the deceased had left specific instructions that he wanted his body to be cremated, there is no legal obligation to carry out his wishes.'

Consumers Association
What to do when someone dies

'Eating people is wrong' and the most taboo of all the taboos about death. Tribes who practiced cannibalism were described as 'depraved' by explorers, who wisely avoided them.

Three years ago some young South Americans were found to have survived for seventy days after a plane crash in the snow-bound Andes. They had clearly been eating *something,* and there was a certain amount of horror expressed when it was learned that they had lived on the flesh of their dead companions. In the book which tells their extraordinary story, the 'first time' is described:

'Most of the bodies were covered by snow, but the buttocks of one protruded a few yards from the plane. With no exchange of words Canessa knelt, bared the skin and cut into the flesh with a piece of broken glass. It was frozen hard and difficult to cut, but he persisted until he had cut away twenty slivers the size of match-sticks. He then went back to the plane and placed them on the roof.

Inside there was silence. The boys cowered in the aircraft. Canessa told them that the meat was there on the roof, drying in the sun, and that those who wished to do so should come out and eat it. No one came, and again Canessa took it on himself to prove his resolution. He prayed to God to help him do what he knew to be right and then took a piece of meat in his hand.

He hesitated. Even with his mind so firmly made up, the horror of the act paralysed him. His hand would neither rise to his mouth nor fall to his side while the revulsion that possessed him struggled with his stubborn will. The will prevailed. The hand rose and pushed the meat into his mouth. He swallowed it. He felt triumphant. His conscience had overcome a primitive taboo. He was going to survive.

Later that evening, small groups of boys came out of the plane to follow his example. Zerbino took a strip and swallowed it as Canessa had done, but it stuck in his throat. He scooped a handful of snow into his mouth and managed to wash it down.'

Piers Paul Read *Alive!*

A photo taken by one of the Andes survivors.

Cremation

STUDENTS of death will have a heaven-sent opportunity to enhance their knowledge on Saturday, March 22, when the doors of Lambeth Crematorium will be thrown open to the public.

"Not a gimmick, but a serious effort to overcome old wives' tales by showing how the crematorium actually works," says Councillor Malcolm Noble, chairman of Lambeth Public Services Committee.

At a busy crematorium there are funeral services at 20—30 minute intervals. To make sure everything runs smoothly, banks of TV sets relay pictures from different parts of the crematorium to a central office where the timing is supervised.

LONDON'S newest crematorium has a special window . through which people can see bodies sliding down a ramp into the furnace. Understandably, few people have taken the opportunity to use the viewing room which holds two people.

A spokesman for the cemetary at Manor Park, which handles 5,000 cremations a year, said: "The process is carried out with dignity. ·

"Onlookers can see the coffin slide down the ramp into the open doors of the furnace.

"The doors close, and that's it."

The coffin moves from the chapel into the furnace. It takes about an hour for the average coffin to burn up. The workers aren't squeamish about the business: 'It's just a job. It doesn't bother us. It's harder on the people upstairs who have to deal with the family.'

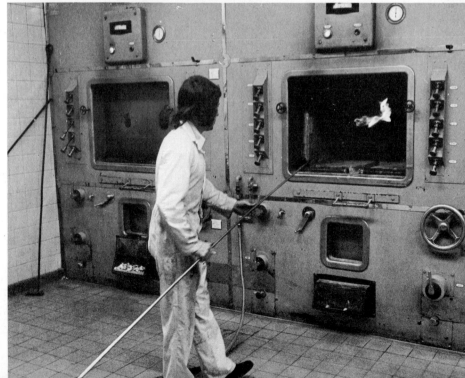

The crematorium chapel, where mourners will see the coffin slide behind curtains on its way to the furnace.

An Open Day visitor gets a close look at a cremator.

HONEYSETT.

53

DEATH and technology

'And to what do you attribute your remarkable long life of a hundred and twenty-one years, Mr. Thilby?'

If you'd asked someone two hundred years ago, whether men could ever avoid death, they'd have told you that there was probably as much chance of living for ever as going to the moon. It has been rubbed into all of us often enough that progress in science and technology has been amazing in the last couple of centuries. And in no area has more been discovered, and achieved, than in that of the human body: how it works and how things stop it working and how to stop them. . . In fact, we know so much, and can do so much, that the very bedrock of belief seems to have altered. Men used to suffer and consider it their fate; they explained the miseries of life, the death of children, the epidemics of smallpox and plague, by their own sin. They survived the misery, if they did survive, by keeping a strong faith in a religion which could explain the continual tragedy to them. We don't live like that at all, now. Men aren't sufferers these days — at least, not if they live in the right corners of the world. Men are conquerors: of the atom, of air, of space. Of death? That may seem far-fetched, but I wonder if the *possibility* of immortality does influence modern feelings about death? Maybe the very inability to talk

about it is significant. After all, if men have mastered so much, maybe they prefer to push out of sight something which so far defeats them.

A friend working in an African school told me this story. One day a student of seventeen or eighteen years old came to the teacher and asked his permission to go home to his village for money. After three days a message arrived at the school that the boy was dead. Since he had been healthy when he set out, my

friend was very shocked. He decided to go to the boy's village to sympathise with his family and find out just what had happened. The elders of the family told how the student had complained of stomach pains and then died. Why hadn't he travelled to hospital? The pain was too severe, and there had been no time. My friend, who is English, questioned for a long time, keen to know the cause of death. The old men shrugged. What was the point? The boy was dead, and no amount of curiosity would change that.

How long will YOU live?

Listed below are some of the conditions and characteristics that can lengthen or shorten your life, according to choice and chance. First, work out your average life expectancy from the table (based on the Registrar General's figures for England and Wales, and the 1972 Statistical Review). Then, add or subtract years according to your answers to the questionnaire. Apart from the table, the quiz is not, of course, scientific. It can only indicate some of the factors involved in life expectancy for the average person. It is, however, founded on sound actuarial and medical opinion.

Present Age	Men	Women			
0	69	75	68–69	79	82
1	70½	76½	70–71	80	83
2	70½	76½	72–73	81	84
3–6	70	77	74–75	82	85
7–30	71	77	76	83	85
31–39	72	77	77–78	84	86
40–45	72	78	79	85	87
46–49	73	78	80	86	87
50–52	73	79	81	86	88
53–56	74	79	82	87	88
57–60	75	79	83	88	89
61–62	76	80	84	89	90
63–65	77	81	85	89	90
66–67	78	82	90	93	94
			100	102	102

If you live in the South-East or West of England, add 3 years.
If you live in Greater London, add 1 year.
If you live in the North or East of England, subtract 1 year.
If you live in Wales, subtract 2 years.
If you live in Scotland, subtract 3 years.

If you have a professional job, add 2 years.
If you are a civil servant, clerk, or secretary, add 1 year.
If you have a skilled job, add nothing.
If you have a partly skilled job, subtract 2 years.
If you have an unskilled job, subtract 5 years.

If friends or relations describe you as always calm, add 5 years.
as usually calm, add 3 years.
as moderately calm, add 1 year.
If friends or relations describe you as moderately tense, subtract 1 year.
as usually tense, subtract 3 years.
as always tense, subtract 5 years.
If you are given to nervous breakdowns, subtract 6 years.

If you are married and under 30, add 5 years.
If you are married and over 30 but under 60, add 2 years.
If you are married and over 60, add nothing.
If you are married, over 40, and have extra-marital affairs, subtract 2 years.
If you are single and under 40, subtract 2 years.
If you are single, divorced, or a widower and over 40, subtract 5 years.
If you are single, over 40, and have more than one lover, subtract 2 years.

If you smoke a pipe or cigars occasionally, subtract 2 years.
If you smoke a pipe or cigars regularly, subtract 3 years.
If you smoke under 20 cigarettes a day, subtract 3 years.
If you smoke 20 cigarettes a day, subtract 4 years.
If you smoke up to 40 cigarettes a day, subtract 6 years.
If you smoke over 40 cigarettes a day, subtract 10 years.

If you drink six tots of spirits or its equivalent a day, subtract 5 years.
If you drink half-a-bottle of spirits or its equivalent a day, subtract 10 years.
If you drink more, subtract 15 years.

If you walk or run four miles a day (or its equivalent), add 3 years.
If you walk or run six miles a day (or its equivalent), add 5 years.
If you never exercise, subtract 5 years.

If you are over 30 and up to half-a-stone overweight, subtract 2 years.
If you are over 30 and up to a stone overweight, subtract 3 years.
If you are over 30 and up to two stone overweight, subtract 5 years.
If you are over 30 and more than two stone overweight, subtract 6 years.

If you never visit your doctor, subtract 1 year.
If you visit your doctor only for regular check-ups, add 2 years.
If you are often ill, subtract 2 years.
If you are under 40 and have false teeth, subtract 3 years.
If you are over 40 and have false teeth, subtract 2 years.
If you are over 50 and have your own teeth, add 2 years.

•If your father lived to be over 70, add 1 year; over 80, add 2 years; over 85, add 3 years. If your mother lived to be over 70, add 1 year; over 80, add 2 years; over 85, add 3 years.

This seemed to show the difference in attitude between people from a highly scientific, technological background, and those whose background could be called 'natural'. In Europe we know why a man dies. Even if he is 99 years old, written on the death certificate will be the *cause* of his death: pneumonia, cardiac failure, or some other long word. And an unexpected death, like that of this student, will be followed by a post-mortem examination of the body. By cutting it open in likely spots, a doctor will try to find out what went wrong. In particularly strange circumstances, a coroner's inquest will hear evidence about the death, to see whether something suspicious led to it.

In London in 1830 the average age at death was estimated at 44 years for gentry, professional persons and their families; at 25 years for tradesmen, clerks and their families, and at 22 years for labourers and their families. In Manchester in 1840 more than 57 out of every hundred working class children died before reaching the age of five. These figures are comparable with those for a poor country like Upper Volta in 1974. But medical science discovered the causes of the child killers, like diphtheria. Improvements in sanitation, housing and hygiene, plus the discoveries of drugs and vaccines and all the rest of the medical revolution of the past century have meant a far longer life expectancy for us.

There are still two big areas in which the battle (it's hard to avoid that sort of word when talking about medical advance) is being waged. These are heart diseases and cancer. The latter has captured the public imagination, and the amount of publicity it receives makes it appear a new phenomenon. But it isn't, it's just that people don't die of the things they once died of, like smallpox, but they do die of cancer. Again relatively few people die of cancer, and quite often they are very old, but since people aren't dying of other things, the cancer patients show up more. Anyway, people are very frightened of cancer, and a great deal of space is given in women's magazines and on the telly, to people who've been cured of it, or haven't been, or think they know how to cure it. And a great deal of the sort of questioning which my friend made of those African elders is going on. Without a doubt the answers will come.

The other challenge is heart disease, the largest single cause of death in the industrialized world. It is frequently aggravated by modern ways of life, where people eat the wrong kinds of food and don't take enough exercise. It is strange to see that the way of life which brought the medical advances also made some of the diseases worse! This is probably true of cancer, too. We know that cigarette smoking, a modern habit, increases chances of getting lung cancer, and modern eating may provoke some stomach cancers. So modern science and technology battle

Diseases and Casualties this year.

Abortive and Stilborne	617	Executed	21	Palsie	30
Aged	1545	Flox and Smal Pox	655	Plague	68596
Ague and Feaver	5257	Found dead in streets, fields, &c.	20	Plannet	6
Appoplex and Suddenly	116	French Pox	86	Plurisie	15
Bedrid	10	Frighted	23	Poysoned	1
Blasted	5	Gout and Sciatica	27	Quinsie	35
Bleeding	16	Grief	46	Rickets	557
Bloudy Flux, Scowring & Flux	185	Griping in the Guts	1288	Rising of the Lights	397
Burnt and Scalded	8	Hangd & made away themselves	7	Rupture	34
Calenture	3	Headmouldshot & Mouldfallen	14	Scurvy	105
Cancer, Gangrene and Fistula	56	Jaundies	110	Shingles and Swine pox	2
Canker, and Thrush	111	Impostume	227	Sores, Ulcers, broken and bruised Limbes	82
Childbed	625	Kild by several accidents	46	Spleen	14
Chrisomes and Infants	1258	Kings Evill	86	Spotted Feaver and Purples	1929
Cold and Cough	68	Leprosie	2	Stopping of the Stomack	332
Collick and Winde	134	Lethargy	14	Stone and Strangury	98
Consumption and Tissick	4808	Livergrowne	20	Surfet	1251
Convulsion and Mother	2036	Meagrom and Headach	12	Teeth and Worms	2614
Distracted	5	Measles	7	Vomiting	51
Dropsie and Timpany	1478	Murthered, and Shot	9	Wenn	1
Drowned	50	Overlaid and Starved	45		

Christned { Males — 5114, Females — 4853, In all — 9967 }

Buried { Males — 48569, Females — 48737, In all — 97306 } Of the Plague — 68596

Increased in the Burials in the 130 Parishes and at the Pest-house this year —— 79009
Increased of the Plague in the 130 Parishes and at the Pest-house this year —— 68590

This is the 'Bill of Mortality' for London in 1665, showing causes of death for that year. 'Plannet' indicates death caused by the influence of the stars. It is interesting to note that 'Grief' was accepted as the cause of 46 deaths.

with problems partly created by modern science and technology. And can you even call them problems when you compare the average life expectancy in Northern Europe: 73 years, with that of Upper Volta: 27 years?

One well-publicized field that throws medical advance into perspective is that of the heart transplant. First of all, the transplanters are working in this popular modern battlefield, so there is a great deal of interest in what they are doing. Also, the whole proceeding is so dramatic, involving the removal of organs from the body of a person who is at the point of death, and putting them in the body of a person who is alive but who will die soon from their weak heart, that it fascinates. And it throws up all sorts of questions, not least the crucial one — when is a dead man dead?

To obtain the heart they need, surgeons are dependent on sudden, violent death, usually in motor accidents. Motor cars are, of course, an example of scientific and technological progress, and you could say that without them we would save the lives without the transplants. And maybe if the pace of life hadn't been accelerated by the motor car and people's weight hadn't increased because they sat in the things instead of walking, then

BACK FROM THE DEAD

City kidney team 'No' to body — then woman patient revived

Evening Mail
Reporter

A WOMAN came back from the dead in a Birmingham hospital after kidney transplant surgeons had refused her body. Today the woman is believed to be alive and well although she was pronounced dead by doctors at the Queen Elizabeth Hospital.

Surgeon Mr. Victor Brookes disclosed the miracle recovery at a meeting of Birmingham Area Health Authority which controls on organ transplants.

He said today: "This occurred more than three years ago. I last saw the lady about three months ago when she came to an out-patient clinic.

"The woman stopped breathing after a major operation for cancer. Checks by experts showed no brain activity."

A respirator was used to keep her body functioning.

It was while she was on the respirator that Mr. Brookes checked with the kidney unit to see if they were interested in her organs.

They turned down the offer and the woman subsequently recovered.

Mr. Brookes, who refused to name the patient, said: "Medicine is not an exact science. It is the only instance of its kind that I have been involved in.

"We should always err on the side of caution.

The authority decided that unless relatives can be traced and their approval obtained no transplant operation can take place.

there wouldn't be so many people with bad hearts. . . Anyway, the heart transplants have begun.

In the following extract, the writer is describing the end of a young girl who has been horribly injured in a road accident. Her brain has been severely damaged. She is being kept alive with drug stimulants, blood transfusions and an artificial respirator, which is breathing for her. The doctor is about to switch off the respirator:

'Yet even then she would not be totally dead, for the separate organs and tissues of her body would die their own particular deaths at separate intervals. Her brain, had it been alive, would go first.

Her liver and adrenals would die next, within an hour. The heart would take from one to two hours – depending a great deal on its temperature. Tissues such as bone, skin, arteries and cornea could be used several hours after death and kept alive much longer under certain conditions, such as freezing.

This extra life-span of organs and tissues was vital in doing a transplant. It allowed time to take the heart, the liver or kidney, from one body and place it in another. It was an extra margin of time which made transplants possible. To ensure this margin the donor had to be kept 'alive' until the last moment.

For this reason I intended to hold Denise Darvall artificially in life until I needed her heart. She would be brought to the operating table while being automatically ventilated, with her heart still beating in

her body. At that point we could take it at any time. Indeed, since brain death had been established, and her heart was kept in life by us, there was no reason why it could not be removed while still beating.'

Christiaan Barnard *One Life*

To people for whom death is a painful but inevitable part of life, like those old Africans I mentioned, this whole concept of death as something a man can switch on or off would be impossible to grasp. I suspect it is impossible for us to grasp, too. Is medical technology charging forward on one front before it has attended to more familiar challenges, in places like Upper Volta? Certainly the transplant operation creates whole new problems, not so much scientific as ethical:

'Is it not a macabre scene when doctors place a patient on the heart-lung machine in an operating room while simultaneously, in a similar room next door, a second team waits, forceps in hand, around a young person fighting against death? These people are not there to help the patient. With feverish eagerness they are waiting to open his defenceless body in order to save someone else.'

Dr Werner Forsmann

and legal:

'A gunman in California is pleading not guilty to murder because the heart from the man he allegedly shot last month was later removed for a transplant. The lawyer for Andrew Lyons, aged 36, told a preliminary hearing that 29-year-old Samuel Allen's heart was still beating when surgeons removed it.

The heart was kept artificially alive, and on 12 September, two days after Mr. Allen's death, it was given to a patient in Salt Lake City.'

Sunday Times

and simply practical:

'A man of 65 who was certified dead by two doctors started breathing again as surgeons who were removing his kidneys for a transplant operation made their first incision. . .'

Guardian

Science may seem to reign, but there are still many stories about the mysterious

deaths of individuals. What about the will to live? Nothing very scientific about that. However, at the present time it is a fact that most surgeons will refuse to operate on a person who is convinced he is going to die even if they believe the person's chances are extremely good. A butcher told me that his grandfather, an old man in his eighties and owner of the business, came into the shop one morning and said to his grandson: 'Right lad, the business is yours.' He then took to his bed, though he'd never had a serious illness in his life, and didn't have one at this time. Within five days he had died. On the other hand a nurse told of a patient, dying from cancer and with a month to live, who hung on until her husband, a student, had got his degree. This meant living for six months longer than expected. She died the day after she heard her good news. The exercise of the human will over life and death is a curious and exciting thought. It is the sort of thought that makes us wonder about death. What *is* it? Merely the end?

Here in the cold bed of death, free from trouble and pain, sleeps at rest, Eliza Bradford, Daughter of Fordyce & Elizabeth Foster, who died *Oct.* 14, 1811. Æt. 14 Months

Monuments and . . .

It's hard to accept that we will be forgotten when we are dead. Living men have always tried to perpetuate their memory in monuments. The Pyramids and the Taj Mahal stand as evidence to this. Some people leave money for ceremonies to keep their memory alive. But do the quaint customs in the photographs opposite have anything to do with the people they are meant to commemorate?

The Taraja in Indonesia place their dead in caves cut into the rock face. When an important person dies a model is made and placed with other figures in special galleries.

The monument to Sir Robert Cecil in Hatfield Church, Hertfordshire: portrait of the man when living, and below him, the decaying corpse.

This Italian stands beside the gravestone he had made ready for his death.

. . . ceremonies

John Knill was the Mayor of St. Ives in 1767. He died in 1797. In his will he made provision that every five years, on St. James' day, ten girls under the age of ten should dance to a fiddler for a quarter of an hour in front of the mausoleum he had built for himself. They were to be dressed in white and they would receive £5 each. They were to be accompanied by two widows over the age of sixty-four who would receive £2 each. He also provided for £5 to be allotted to a married couple over the age of sixty, the husband being a fisherman, seaman, labourer or tinner, who had brought up the largest family without any assistance from the parish. £5 was allotted to the best local net worker and the same sum is now given to the best packer of pilchards for export.

Two ladies with the bags of flour they have been given under an 800-year-old bequest made in the Hampshire village of Tichbourne.

The END

This is the Question. What happens next? Is death an end, or is there more? The most tantalising idea in the world is of the man who comes back from the dead, and can answer the question. In the course of writing this book I did meet a man whose heart had stopped during an operation, but sadly he could say nothing; he didn't remember a thing. And we already know that the stoppage of the heart doesn't mean complete death, so perhaps this man hadn't been dead after all. There is a story of a Russian soldier, Cherepanov, who was killed in action in 1944. His body was still well preserved after three days, and a strange Professor, by complicated experiments, managed to resurrect him. How true this tale is I don't know. Maybe the man hadn't really been dead when the body was brought to the Professor. . .? Maybe the whole thing was a con-trick? Cherepanov wrote about that time:

'Doctors and friends often ask me how it feels to have been dead. They seem to expect a startling answer. When I tell them the truth: that I was wounded, fell asleep and later woke up again, they are disappointed. But that's how it was to me. .

The only other thing I do remember is a feeling of happiness and well-being — the sort of feeling you had when you were small, had been away for school camp and were then pleased to be going home again. . .

But if it was death I experienced, it was by no means the dramatic experience we have always held it to be. It was a calm and contented thing.'

Well, that's quite comforting, but we've no way of knowing if it's *true.* Nor will we, until we die, and then we won't *know;* knowing being something that living people can claim. It's truly a mystery, and a frightening one. Sigmund Freud said that 'no one believes in his own death; and in the unconscious everyone is convinced of his own immortality.' But death is still the inescapable fact, whatever our minds, or medical progress might try to otherwise suggest. Life expectancy may have risen, but old people now don't seem any older than old people used to be. Stop smoking and avoid lung cancer. But you'll die just the same in the end. A Belgian doctor believes that people will soon be able to live for hundreds of years. He is the co-president of the International Association for the Artificial Prolongation of the Human Specific Lifespan. He claims that he will live until he is 500 years old. At the moment he is 45.

Heenan: What I'll do in Heaven

SEVERAL TIMES in the past 10 years Cardinal Heenan, who died on Friday, suffered severe illnesses and came close to death. Twice he received the Last Rites of the Roman Catholic Church. In 1970 MURIEL BOWEN talked to him at length about Heaven and how he saw life after the grave. The interview was not to be published until after the Cardinal's death.

‘ I was about seven when I first started to look forward to going to Heaven. I can honestly say I have looked forward to it all my life. But I have not made many plans. That's the great thing about eternity—you're not rushed off your feet making plans with one eye on the clock.

But to start, I know exactly what I want to do. For the first 100 years I want to thank God from the bottom of my heart for being there. After all, in different circumstances I might have gone to the other place. . .

I often hope that Heaven will be like a one-class ship, that there will be areas where everybody can meet. The Gospel says that in my Father's house there will be many mansions; that worries me a bit. There will be family and friends in the better mansions and one of the joys of Heaven must surely be to meet them again. My mother, for instance—she was a saint, a great saint I think now when I remember my father's temper! She will be higher up than I will be; I'm certain of that.

The great thing is that there will be time; time to meet old friends. Pope John, for instance.

Pay now—die later

WE HAVE hesitated to pass on this tip before, for fear of being thought macabre. But, just as it is prudent to write a will while yet hale and hearty, so perhaps it is to make burial arrangements.

Last September, the Department of the Environment sent a circular to local authorities advising them to reconsider their charges for cremation and burial. It seems likely that many will soon be revising them. Bradford is an example, as reader Mrs Margaret McGowan points out. The council there tells us that from April 1, a grave space (for up to three relatives) will be going up from £21 to £65. If you buy now, it will give you rights on the plot for 100 years. The cost of an ordinary grave, with no rights as to its position, will go up from £15 to £24. If you later decide you do not want to be buried in Bradford, or wherever, you could assign the rights to somebody else.

Cheating death is an idea to play with. Our own lives would be quite different if they were endless. Think of all the drives you wouldn't need if you weren't going to die: reproduction, for one! Perhaps infinite life would be infinitely boring. . . Anyway, there's no chance of it at the moment, and maybe there never will be. What's for sure is that we are all going to die. And it might help us if we try to face the fact, think about it a little. Ignoring it isn't going to make it go away.

'All right, so you're an atheist! So you're going to be re-cycled!'

Stanley Spencer's painting of Resurrection Day when the graves open and the dead ascend to Judgement.